GENESIS SECRETS REVEALED

PRIMEVAL

Fallen Angels
131 Franklin Plaza, Box 204
Franklin, NC 28734

CK Quarterman

GENESIS SECRETS REVEALED PRIMEVAL

CK QUARTERMAN

No element of this publication may be reproduced, stored in a retrieval system, nor transmitted in any form or means without either the prior written permission of the publisher, or author. This includes electronic, mechanical, photocopying, recording, scanning, or otherwise; except as permitted under Section 107 or 108 of the 1976 United States Copyright Act. Requests to the publisher for reprint permission should be addressed to:

CK Quarterman

131 Franklin Plaza

P.O. Box 204

Franklin, NC 28734

www.author@genesissecretsrevealed.com

ISBN- 1480161497

Cover Art by Greg Martin - www.artofgregmartin.com

Quotations are from the King James Bible, the Orthodox Jewish Bible, or the EW Bullinger Companion Bible unless otherwise noted.

Printed in the United States of America.

Acknowledgments

This book would not have been possible without the support of my friends. I want to extend a special thanks to Dan Mask and my dear wife, Beth. I also thank my readers who honor me by taking time out of their busy lives to read this book.

Hell's Fiery Grasp & God's Eternal Love

The Creator became the creature, to destiny bear, the law's demand, for sin to atone, that God might be alone, only Him having atoned. Suffer He must, sin and anguish burdened, hell's destiny for so much. Judgment must prevail in hell's fiery grasp! God's soul must atone for judgment past. My sin must prevail, to judgment obtain. The soul of God travail He did, and answered law's demand. Cursed was He at God's command. Lightened are we at justice's demand. Sins no longer to bear, and mourned by He who must dare. So suffered He did. Upward He arose. Judgment satisfied. Love shown and sin atoned! The soul of God destined up from hell's fiery grasp at last. (Based upon the Apostle's Creed of 390AD) CK Quarterman

TABLE OF CONTENTS

PROLOGUE 1
WHAT IS IN A NAME 7
WHAT ELOHIM DOES NEXT 14
RUIN-RESTORATION 17
ANCIENT HIGH TECHNOLOGY 27
COSMOS 33
THE FIRMAMENT 44
MANKIND 50
LIFE IN THE GARDEN 58
CAIN AND ABLE 82
GENERATIONS OF ADAM 94
SONS OF GOD 98
NOAH 113
THE FLOOD 120
TOWER OF BABEL 135
AUTHORS BIOGRAPHY 140

PROLOGUE

There is a principle which is a bar against all information, which is proof against all argument, and which cannot fail to keep man in everlasting ignorance. That principle is condemnation before investigation. ~ Edmund Spencer

In **Genesis Secrets Revealed**, I draw back the curtain concealing some of life's greatest mysteries. This book is written for the layperson, not the theologian. Although, I endeavor to be as precise as possible, please keep in mind an entire book could be written about one verse. I will concentrate on conveying the picture in ways that it has never before been presented.

History

According to Jesus, Moses wrote the Book of Genesis (Matthew 19:7, KJV). Therefore, Genesis is not the product of some complex literary process taking place in response to the Babylonian captivity and exile.

The Book of Genesis ("beginning") is the first book of the Hebrew Bible (Tanakh) and the first book of the Christian Old Testament.

Languages. In order to understand Genesis you must first understand the nuances of Hebraic and Semitic languages. In order to enlighten the reader we will look into some of the differences and distinctness of the Hebrew language as they apply to verses in order to see a deeper meaning that we might not ordinarily comprehend in English.

By holding to a Biblical Christianity viewpoint, I exegete (explain scripture) in a literal, grammatical and historical method. I have championed historical texts and extensively used them as well. However, it remains necessary to clear the air on how to use extra Biblical texts.

Extra Biblical texts. We just do not allow them to create doctrine, meaning that where they disagree with Scripture (the 66 books of the Cannon) we just ignore them. Some books like Jasher have interesting things, but depart from the basics of scriptural doctrine.

However, books such as Enoch and Jubilees are much more reliable, but still are not Cannon in the larger Church, though there is an exception with the Ethiopian Church.

All arguments made here are backed by scripture, and "colored" with historical texts, archeology, and extra Biblical material. I believe that it is inherent to explain solely with scripture from the Bible because scripture defines scripture. God gave The Word for the purpose of enabling mankind to develop an understanding of the issues. *"All scripture is given by inspiration of God, and is profitable for doctrine, for reproof, for correction, for instruction in righteousness"* (2 Timothy 3:16, KJV). This simply means that the entire Bible is important from Genesis through Revelation.

Genesis is essential to truly understanding the Bible. The entire Bible rests on the foundation of Genesis; it forms part of all subsequent inspiration. Furthermore, the cosmogony of Genesis is a direct contradiction to that of the world's creation myths. Genesis is an account of Divine creative actions, not myths.

Mythology. Society corrupted the primitive truth by traditionally handing down untrue stories. For example, Greek mythology claims that Prometheus was spared imprisonment in Tartarus and given the task of creating man out of mud. Athena (daughter of Zeus) then breathed life into man's clay figure (Greek playwright Aeschylus).

Interestingly, the Greeks speak of several ages of creation. In the first age, the "deathless gods" dwelt on Olympus and made a golden race of mortal men while Cronos reigned in heaven. They lived like gods without sorrowful hearts; remote and free from toil as well as grief. Miserable age rested not on them. Furthermore, their legs and arms never failed, plus, merry feasting reached beyond all evils. The earth gave them abundant fruit and good things, without stint. They also dwelt in ease with peace upon their lands, richness of flocks, and love by the blessed gods. When they died, it was as though sleep just overcame them.

In the final age, Zeus created men who were warlike and used bronze armor; this was the last generation of men who were destroyed by the flood in the days of Prometheus' son Deucalion.

The strong resemblance of the Genesis creation narrative should be obvious to the reader, as many myths have this as the basis of their creation story.

When composing the "primeval history" of Genesis it might seem that the writer drew on Greek and Mesopotamian sources. This included editing and adding to them in order to create a unified work that fit his theological agenda. I reject this concept.

Genesis is sometimes considered as being mythological. However, it is not mythological, but truth that was written in a historical language. Thus, the mythological similarities to the Book of Genesis that are found in other literature are merely fairy tales distorting the real account contained within Genesis. The purpose of the Genesis' writer is not to write the history of the world, or that of mankind, but to tell the history of redemption.

Modern Critics. Modern critics believe that Genesis came from four sources. Those include the Yahwist, the Elohist, the Deuteronomist and the Priestly source, with each presenting the same basic story joined together by various editors.

I reject the view of modern criticism and believe God revealed himself to mankind by using different names. He did this as a means to detail the differences in his covenant dealings with mankind. In Genesis 1:1, God first revealed Himself as Elohim, and later as Lord God; showing mankind in a distinct covenant relationship to himself.

WHAT IS IN A NAME

"In the beginning (rê'shîyth) *God* ('ĕlôhîym) *created* (bârâ') *the heaven* (shâmayim shâmeh) *and the earth* ('erets)." (Genesis 1:1, KJV)

    The first book of the Bible, Genesis, opens with a statement, "In the beginning God created the heavens and the earth" (Genesis 1:1, KJV). When reading this, one thinks the Bible is telling about the first thing God did; however, it is not! The Bible unabashedly opens with the fact that God exists.

Beginning (rê'shîyth) - principal thing (Hebrew)

God ('ĕlôhîym) – Elohim (Hebrew)

    Genesis makes no bones about His existence. It states, "Principal thing Elohim". Therefore, we must take this at face value. There was nothing in existence before God, and then we are told God created. There is much we can learn in this first verse, let us look at it in the Hebrew.

Elohim and EL

Elohim is plural. Why use a plural for a single god, in addition, why this odd plural form of Elohim. The name Elohim is unique to Hebraic thinking and is quite rare in the Hebrew language. No other Semitic language uses this word. The masculine plural ending does not mean "gods" when referring to the true God of Israel. When Elohim relates to a singular being (the true God or a false god), it takes a singular verb. References to more than one entity, as in the heavenly powers or the human judges, are when it takes a plural verb. However, when considering the Trinity, that form indeed allows for the plurality within the Godhead which is revealed in the New Testament.

This word's identification of God, angels, man, and idols can only be understood correctly by remembering the root word "El" means power; including in the Canaanite or proto-Semitic languages (Theological Wordbook of the Old Testament). In such light, it is clear that the Hebrews applied the name Elohim to the true God because it conveyed one of his attributes – power. Therefore, the best understanding of Elohim is, "the all-powerful one."

The name El, which in plural form is Elohim, has to do with the first experience that people had of nature's power. El is also the Ugarit term for god. When used of the true God of Israel, El is usually qualified by additional words that further define the meaning and distinguish him from false gods. These other names for God are sometimes called "construct forms," such as Elohei Kedem, God of the beginning. On the other hand, "eternal God," is used in Deuteronomy 33:27 (KJV). Elohim is also often accompanied by the article ha-, meaning "the." Interestingly, Elohim is used over 7000 times in the Hebrew Old Testament. Elohim has the two letters "Aleph Tav", the first and last letters of the Hebrew alphabet as a grammatical marker. It reminds one of Christ in the Book of Revelation stating that He is the Alpha and the Omega (1:8, KJV).

To better understand the word Elohim we need to look at Psalm 82:1:

"Elohim has taken his place in the assembly of EL, in the midst of the Elohim He holds judgment."

The Syriac version renders it, "In the congregation of angels"

In this psalm, God takes his place as leader of the divine council. The psalmist pictures God standing in the "assembly of El," where he accuses the angels of failing to promote justice on earth and carry out their responsibilities (Genesis 6:4). God pronounces sentence upon them by announcing that those angels will die like men. Their fate for unfairness and wickedness means they will also be cast into the Lake of Fire on Judgment Day.

The Congregation. The New Testament gives some insight into the Assembly known as the Congregation:

> *I saw a throne in heaven, and the Ancient of Days sat upon the throne. The throne was similar in appearance to jasper and rubies, and there was a rainbow around the throne, in appearance like an emerald. Around the throne were twenty-four thrones, and on the thrones I saw the twenty-four elders sitting, in white robes; and on their heads were crowns of gold.*
>
> *And from the throne proceeded lightnings, voices and thunders. Seven torches of fire were burning before the throne; and before the throne was*

> *something like a sea of glass, similar to crystal.*
>
> *And in the midst of the throne, and around the throne, were four living beings. The first living being was like a lion, the second living being was like a calf, the third living being had a face of a man, and the fourth living being was like a flying eagle. And the four living beings, each one having six wings apiece, were full of eyes around and within. And before the throne was a golden altar (Revelation 4:1-10 Paraphrased).*

This is called the Congregation (Assembly). The name arrives from the many which stand before it, an uncounted amount, because of the multitudes in attendance. Council is called the Congregation several times. Below is a smaller picture of the "Divine Council" in action as found in I Kings 22: 20-22:

> *And the Ancient of Days said, "Who shall entice this king that he may go and be defeated at Ramoth Gilead?" And one said on this manner; and another said on that manner. And there came forth*

another, and stood before the Ancient of Days, and said, "I will convince him."

And the Ancient of Days said to him, "Wherewith?" And he said, "I will go, and will be a lying spirit in the mouth of all his prophets." And he said, "You will convince him, go now, and do so" and one said, on that manner and another.

These were members of the counsel. Realistically, the Ancient of Days did not need advice, but none the less he chose to surround himself with others who were called the Elohim. He said in 2 Chronicles 18:18,

Therefore hear the word of the LORD; I saw the LORD sitting upon his throne, and all the host of heaven standing on his right hand and on his left.

Here the "host of heaven" (tzeva' hashamayim) stands before the Ancient of Days. Clearly, this speaks of angelic beings, including those on the heavenly divine council. Before time began and prior to creation in Genesis 1:1, (referred to as from everlasting to everlasting) there was the Ancient of Days who sat at the head of the Council with the twenty four elders and others.

To reiterate, there was nothing in the beginning except the principal thing, God. He stood at the head of the Assembly and was the all-powerful one. All this is reflected in the Bible's use of the word Elohim.

WHAT ELOHIM DOES NEXT

"In the beginning (rê'shîyth) God ('ĕlôhîym) created (bârâ') the heaven (shâmayim shâmeh) and the earth ('erets)." (Gen 1:1)

He created – bara (Hebrew)

The heaven - shâmayim shâmeh (Hebrew)

Earth - 'erets (Hebrew)

Create

Heaven and Earth are straight forward, but "bara" is not. "Create" (bara in Hebrew) means to call forth out of nothingness. We get the Christian doctrine "Ex nihilo" a Latin phrase meaning "out of nothing" from this Hebrew word. Subsequently, further in the text, the word "make" or "form" (asah in Hebrew) denotes a re-fashioning or production from pre-existing material (this is not the same as "bara" meaning to make from out of nothing). Creation occurred "ex deo", or out of the very substance of God. Everything that exists is because God created it with his very own substance and nature.

There was no darkness, void or non-existent space. Elohim made the universes by mere will of having them appear, without any use of pre-existent matter.

God's Existence. God is eternal and exists outside of time and space. He is the *"high and lofty One who inhabits eternity"* (Isaiah 57:15 KJV). Time was created along with the universe and began at a finite point "Creatio Ex Nihilo" out of nothingness with the "Big-Bang." To the casual observer, the moment of creation appears as a single point of energy or singularity. This is the result of having the entire cosmos compressed into God's words; hence the "Big-Bang" Model of the universe. When God spoke the words they exploded into all known and unknown elements, including the fires of the suns, the darkness, and the cold. Neither darkness nor light existed before creation Ex Nihilo. God made the cosmos by mere will of having it exist.

Time is something that is exclusive to this dimension in which we live. Eternity is not bound by time. God lives in eternity which has no beginning and no end. Before time, there was only eternity, and for God eternity is a never-ending present.

In summary, we understand that Elohim was the principal thing with no beginning and no end. Secondly, he created the heavens and the earth out of nothingness. We will see in the next chapter why the Hebrew makes such a distinction between bara and asah. It is a very important feature of Genesis that these two different words are used in the creation story.

RUIN-RESTORATION

"And the earth was without form, and void; and darkness was upon the face of the deep. And the Spirit of God moved upon the face of the waters." (Gen. 1:2)

The Ruin-Reconstruction Theory suggests that there is a gap of time between a distinct creation event in the first verse of Genesis and the second recreation in the second verse of Genesis, explaining the age of the Earth.

And the earth was (**hâyâh**) without form, (**tôhû**) and void; (**bôhû**) and darkness (**chôshek**) was upon the face of the deep.(**tehôm tehôm**) And the Spirit (**rûach**) of God (**'ĕlôhîym**) moved (**râchaph**) upon the face of the waters. (Gen 1:2 Hebrew)

hâyâh - become, come to pass, became

tôhû - desolation, or become worthless.

bôhû - ruin

chôshek - destruction

tehôm tehôm - abyss

rûach - breath

râchaph – to brood as a mother hen

The Ruin-Reconstruction theory, known as Gap Creation, suggests a time lapse exists between a distinct creation event in Genesis' first verse and the second recreation that takes place in the second verse, explaining the Earth's age. This concept suggests that science has proven the Earth is much older than accounted for by adding up biblical chronology.

Furthermore, the Ruin-Reconstruction theory maintains the Genesis Creation account is inerrant in scientific fact. Gap Creationists assert that the biblical account lapse lasted an unknown number of years (between a first creation in Genesis 1:1 and a second recreation in Genesis 1:2). This allows for various observations, including; determining the Earth's age as well as that of the universe, dinosaurs, oil formation, ice ages, and geological formations that occurred as outlined by science without contradicting a literal belief in Genesis.

In contrast, the Ruin-Reconstruction theory differs from "Day-age Creationism" and "Young Earth creationism."

Day-age creationism claims that the days of creation were much longer (thousands or millions of years). Young Earth Creationism, although it agrees concerning the six literal 24-hour days of creation, does not suggest a time gap.

The Ruin-Reconstruction concept alleges that a cataclysmic judgment was pronounced upon the earth (between the 1st and 2nd verse) due to the fall of Lucifer. In addition, other verses of Genesis describe a reforming of the earth from a chaotic state. The E.W. Bullinger Companion Bible of 1909 clearly shows the Ruin – Restoration theme of Genesis:

> *The beginning God **(prepared, formed, fashioned,** and) created the Heavens and the earth **(Perfect, complete and to be Inhabited**). And the earth became waste, and void; and darkness was upon the face of the deep **(Frozen Ice**). And the Spirit of God moved **(hovering, brooding**); [the beginning of the heavens and earth which are now] upon the face of the waters [**Melted Ice**].* (Gen. 1:1-2, EWB-CB)

The six days of Genesis are the account of a re-creation, or regeneration of a previously existent heavens and earth (not the original creation), and seven creative days within Genesis chapter one are not a geological history of the earth!

Ruin-Reconstruction relies upon specific linguistic reasoning behind the Hebrew Scriptures. First, a newly created earth should not have been without form and void. Second, the word "was" in Genesis 1:2 is more accurately translated as "became." The Hebrew word for "was" is haw-yaw' and means "become", or come to pass. Third, "create" and "made" are different in the Hebrew language as well. "Create" (bara in Hebrew) means to call forth out of nothingness. The Christian doctrine "Ex nihilo" has a Latin phrase meaning "out of nothing" from this Hebrew word. Subsequently in the text, the words "make" or "form" (asah in Hebrew) mean a re-fashioning or making from pre-existing material. This refers to the substance remaining after the earth underwent Lucifer's judgment.

Hebrews 11:3 says, *"By faith we understand that the worlds were framed by the word of God, so that the things which are seen were not made of things which are visible."*

This means that the heavens and the earth came into existence by divine command and was not assembled from pre-existing matter or energy. Further support can be seen in Isaiah 45:18 where it is stated that the earth was not created in "vain" (tohu), "*He* (God) *formed* (asah) *it* (the earth) *to be inhabited.*" The word "was" or "became" in Genesis 1:2, allows a change of state to occur from verse one to verse two and is more accurately translated "became". That is, the initial perfect creation of verse one "became" without form and void, indicating a transition occurred. Genesis 1:2 reveals that,

"And the earth was (**had become**) *without form, and void; and darkness was upon the face of the deep. And the Spirit of God moved upon the face of the waters."* (Genesis 1:2)

Additional support comes from the phrase *"without form and void."*

Consider other Biblical texts in which these words are found together. In Isaiah 24:1 and Jeremiah 4:23, one sees that they are judgmental in character and context.

Jeremiah describes a time when the earth was *"without form, and void."* Noah's flood was not even as horrific nor brought such barren conditions as described by Jeremiah. It can only be a cataclysmic destruction by God of the Pre-Adamic world. Remember, Isaiah 45:18 states:

*"God did not create the earth **in vain**; he formed it in order for it to be inhabited".*

Jeremiah also wrote:

> *I beheld the earth, and, lo, it was without **form, and void**; and the heavens, and they had no light. I beheld the mountains, and, lo, they trembled, and all the hills moved lightly. I beheld, and, lo, there was **no man**, and all the birds of the heavens were fled. I beheld, and, lo, the fruitful place was a wilderness, and all the cities thereof were broken down at the presence of the LORD, and by his fierce anger. For thus hath the LORD said, The whole land shall be desolate; yet will I not make a full end.*

*For this shall the earth mourn, and the heavens above be black: because I have spoken it, I have purposed it, and will not repent, neither will I turn back from it (*Jeremiah *4:23-28).*

There were no descendants of Adam (no man), yet there were cities that God destroyed by his wrath – who dwelt in these cities? According to Hebrew Cosmogony, Earth was changed by catastrophe, before the birth of our world as we know it. Worlds were shaped and brought into existence, only to be destroyed in the course of time, not to be inhabited by man. He made several worlds before ours, but he destroyed them all. Hebrew mythology assigns this to a period before Adam and different geophysical catastrophes. It should also be noted that DNA remains actually older than 6,000 years (like "Neanderthal" and "Cro-Magnon") will be found to have no genetic connection to any people living on the Earth today.

Questions answered by the Ruin-Reconstruction theory include: (1) How can the Earth only be 6,000 years old, according to the Bible's chronology, when the forensic evidence of geology and the fossil records reveal that the Earth is very ancient?

(2) How could death have only started with the fall of man at about 6,000 years ago when evidence for death is found in the Pleistocene geologic era, and a long reign of death across ancient ages past? (3) How can man have been on the Earth for only about 6,000 years when there is evidence of man-like creatures inhabiting the Earth for hundreds of thousands of years? What happened during this Gap between Genesis 1:1 and 1:2?

One also wonders, what took place during this time gap between Genesis 1:1 and 1:2. Around the Cambrian geologic period (about 500-600 million years ago), an explosion of death happened to well-developed life forms in the fossil record, with no antecedent fossils in the more ancient Precambrian, except for what could be primitive cell remains. Consequently, what appears in the fossil record as an explosion of life was actually an explosion of death. Living things do not leave remains until they die. The Cambrian geologic period marks the first record of death and the fall of Lucifer. Because Lucifer was the steward of the whole creation under heaven when he fell, all things under his rule were also subjected to corruption.

Adam's sin brought death into our world (Romans 5:12). Therefore, it is no contradiction with the Bible that Earth's geology shows an ancient track record of death on this planet long before Adam. As seen throughout the geologic record, there is evidence of mass extinction and geologic catastrophes.

Recapping, in Gen. 1:1, the word created is baw-raw' and means to create out of nothing. After, Gen. 1:1 the word "made" is used but it is a different word in Hebrew, known as aw-saw,' and means "to make out of existent materials." This is translated as made instead of create so the reader knows it is a different assertion.

In verse one of Genesis, God created. Thereafter, God made or recreated from existent material the Earth from material he had created out of nothingness in the first verse.

The science behind both Carbon and Argon data is flawed, but not by millions of years. Carbon and Argon dating based upon radioactive decay may have been accelerated in the recent past. However, the vast age assigned to the earth based on radioactive measurements can by no means be set aside.

Is there another reasonable explanation for a literal six-day creation that explains the great age of the earth? Perhaps, if one is willing to say that science is very wrong and that the earth is not but 10,000 years old, and that God is tricking the scientists. Many Christians champion a six-day creation, Ex nihilo. In order to do so, one has to deny the geological evidence of the Earth's vast age. Furthermore, no scriptures warrant an arbitrary assumption that a day is more than 24 hours long. Believing that a day is 24 hours is a general principle in the absence of any statement to other effect. Therefore, one must except the days of Genesis are literal 24 hour days.

Thus, Ruin-Restoration Creationism best fits the overall understanding of the creative acts of Elohim. In summary, Elohim existed and created the earth perfectly (Genesis1:1), but it became a wasteland because of war in the heavens (Genesis 1:2). Elohim then remade the earth out of the old materials of the previous creation in a literal six-day period. Ruin-Restoration Creationism proves that the Biblical story of creation is in harmony with the teachings of modern science, and this casts a new light on the integrity of the Bible.

ANCIENT HIGH TECHNOLOGY

Perhaps one of the most extraordinary theological concepts in the Bible is the proposition that God created and destroyed an ancient civilization on earth eons before the time of Adam and Eve. However, the Bible says nothing about how long ago all of this took place, it does seem to indicate that a pre-Adamite society did exist at one time in the distant past as we have explained in the previous chapter. Isaiah gives us additional information for support:

> *How art thou fallen from heaven, O Lucifer, son of the morning! how art thou cut down to the ground, which* **didst weaken the nations!** *For thou hast said in thine heart, I will ascend into heaven, I will exalt my throne above the stars of God: I will sit also upon the mount of the congregation, in the sides of the north: I will ascend above the heights of the clouds; I will be like the most High. Yet thou shalt be brought down to hell, to the sides of the pit.*

They that see thee shall narrowly look upon thee, and consider thee, saying, Is this the man that made the earth to tremble, that did shake kingdoms;

That made the world as a wilderness, and destroyed the cities thereof; that opened not the house of his prisoners? (Isa 14:12-17)

This passage indicates that there were nations of people, pre-humans, and angels inhabiting Earth at the time Lucifer rebelled. The phrase, *"which didst weaken the nations,"* gives credence to such thought.

Jeremiah, as seen in the last chapter, refers to the earth immediately after Pre-Adamite destruction. His account of the annihilation of the Pre-Adamite Earth, where its inhabitants dwelt in cities, must have been between Genesis 1:1 and Genesis 1:2; perhaps meaning to destroy any evidence of the sinfulness of its occupants. However, over the past several decades, there have steadily been an increasing number of archaeological discoveries. Because of their mysterious and highly controversial nature, those findings have been classified as 'out-of-place' artifacts (Ooparts).

Ooparts are objects and artifacts that are found in the wrong place and in an incorrect time line of geological strata, which gives evidence of a Pre-Adamite Earth. Their appearances in these layers of geological strata (which are very ancient) give non-traditional science evidence of a preceding period of technical sophistication extending far beyond the inventive capabilities of the ancient peoples among whose remains they were discovered. As ancient artifacts arise and baffle orthodox science, one can systematically look for clues in these anomalies or Ooparts. Clearly, a pattern indicates that primitive civilizations had highly advanced science and engineering systems; the pyramids of Egypt are among the most enduring and obvious evidence of this. The pyramids show a highly advanced system of science and engineering. Other clues have come from ancient cities discovered off the coasts of Japan, Cuba, Indonesia, and India indicating highly advanced technologies.

The Indian Mahabharata even gives a clue in its poetic description of a nuclear bombing. Although it was written nearly two thousand years ago and handed down by word of mouth from ancient times, it describes the Vimana, known as flying machines.

Furthermore, it depicts wars where terrible weapons are used.

> Gurkha, flying in his swift and powerful Vimana, hurled against the three cities of the Vrishnis and Andhakas a single projectile charged with all the power of the universe. An incandescent column of smoke and fire, as brilliant as ten thousand suns, rose in all its splendor. It was the unknown weapon, the iron thunderbolt, a gigantic messenger of death, which reduced to ashes the entire race of the Vrishnis and Andhakas. The corpses were so burnt they were no longer recognizable. Hair and finger nails fell out, Pottery broke without cause. Foodstuffs were poisoned. To escape, the warriors threw themselves in streams to wash themselves and their equipment. (Mahabarata texts)

Another clue is an ancient artifact reported in the June 1951 Scientific American. A report was given concerning a metallic vase that had been dynamited out of solid rock in Dorchester, Massachusetts and it said:

On putting the two parts together it formed a bell-shaped vessel, 4 1/2 inches high, 6 1/2 inches at the base, 2 1/2 inches at the top and about an eighth of an inch in thickness.

The body of the vessel resembles zinc in color, or a composition metal in which there is a considerable portion of silver. On the sides there are six figures of a flower, a bouquet, beautifully inlaid with pure silver, and around the lower part of the vessel, a vine, or wreath, inlaid also with silver. The chasing, carving and inlaying were done by a craftsman. This unknown object was blown out of solid rock, fifteen feet below the surface. (Scientific American (volume 7, pages 298-299)

An additional ancient artifact find was presented in 1886 by a scientific journal. The periodical published confirmation that an Austrian foundry had discovered a block of coal in which was a small metal cube and it was from the Tertiary period (the period of geologic time, 65 million to 1.6 million years ago).

When tested, the cube was identified as being composed of a steel-nickel alloy. The edges of this ancient cube were perfectly straight and sharp; four of its sides were flat, while the two remaining opposite sides were convex. A deep groove had been machined all the way around the cube as well. It appeared that the entire cube had been made by a machine and was part of a larger mechanism.

Texas has another ancient artifact in its possession at the Creation Evidences Museum; this relic is a metal hammer, imbedded in rock, with a portion of the handle still in place. The hammer was discovered during June 1936, in England. At the time of the discovery, the rock encased the entire metal hammer. A laboratory analyzed the artifact and found that the metal hammerhead was made of 96.6% iron, 0.74% sulphur, and 2.6% chlorine. No metallurgist today can alloy metallic iron with chlorine. The creation of this hammer required technology that cannot be duplicated today.

COSMOS

The Message Bible describes it the best:

"Earth was a soup of nothingness, a bottomless emptiness, an inky blackness" (Genesis 1:2 Message Bible).

Before the six-day recreation of Genesis, the Earth was a dead and desolate planet, drifting in the freezing night of space. Earth was an underwater-uninhabitable planet wandering in the cold and dark remains of an old creation. The land was submerged and the water's angry wrath abounded. Abyss called unto abyss. The lonely night got ever darker, longing for the dawn that did not appear. As a lifeless chunk of rock, the World hurried through the cosmos without any sun to warm its waters or touch its lifeless mass.

One questions what caused the Earth to be in this terrible condition. Remember the fact that it had to be remade, but we did not discuss what had happened to cause this destruction. Briefly review Genesis 1:2, again for clarity.

*"And the earth was **(hâyâh)** without form, **(tôhû)** and void ;**(bôhû)** and darkness **(chôshek)** was upon the face of the deep"* (Genesis 1:2 Hebrew)

hâyâh - become, come to pass, became.

tôhû - desolation, or become worthless.

bôhû - ruin.

chôshek - destruction.

A great destruction took place as described by the author of Genesis and later by Jeremiah. This destruction occurred at the fall of Lucifer. We can see from the Hebrew words that destruction took place upon the earth, but I would submit that this entire Solar System fell under judgment. Before continuing, allow me to paraphrase Genesis 1:2 and clarify where this is going.

"And the earth became a desolation a worthless ruin and destruction was over its entire face". (My paraphrase)

This took place not by accident, for God created the world in Genesis 1:1, so we can presume that he created it whole and protected it. Such destruction came by the hand of God, as told by Jeremiah and Isaiah.

Before Lucifer rebelled, there was trade between the planets (Ezekiel 28:13). The members of the Congregation (Assembly) traded among themselves. When Lucifer ruled over the planets, he ruled over all interplanetary trade.

Ezekiel writes,

> ***In much buying and selling you turned violent***, *you sinned! I threw you, disgraced, off the mountain of God. I threw you out--you, the anointed angel-cherub. No more strolling among the **gems of fire** for you!* (Ezekiel 28:16 MSG)

The Message Bible above is much clearer in this passage than the King James. Look at it in the King James with the help of the Hebrew below:

*"By the multitude of thy **merchandise** (rᵉkûllâh) they have filled the midst of thee with violence."* (Ezekiel 28:16)

rᵉkûllâh – trade, traffic as in peddling.

Lucifer was filled with the kind of "pride" that is called "mafia mentality."

He desired to extend his personal rule beyond what was given to him; hence, falling into this mafia mentality. Basically, he yearned to reach beyond the stars to rule all the material and spiritual realms himself!

Satan is portrayed as ruler of the nations on Earth. This passage shows that there were nations of people inhabiting the Earth at the time of his rebellion. The phrase, *"which didst weaken the nations,"* makes it quite clear.

> *How art thou fallen from heaven, O Lucifer, son of the morning! how art thou cut down to the ground,* **which didst weaken the nations**! *For thou hast said in thine heart, I will ascend into heaven, I will exalt my throne above the stars of God: I will sit also upon the mount of the congregation, in the sides of the north: I will ascend above the heights of the clouds; I will be like the most High. Yet thou shalt be brought down to hell, to the sides of the pit. They that see thee shall narrowly look upon thee, and consider thee, saying, Is this the man that made the earth to tremble, that did shake kingdoms; That made the world as a wilderness, and destroyed the cities thereof; that opened not the house of his prisoners? (Isaiah 14:12-17 KJV)*

Thus both Jeremiah and Isaiah confirm this Pre-Adamite world that *"then was."* Before Adam, civilizations of angels existed on the Earth and also perhaps on other terrestrial planets. Satan was destroyed from the midst of the "stones of fire "(i.e. the planets, Ezekiel 28:16). Evidence of this exists in such places as the Cydonia section of Mars. A more interesting trip to take is the legend of the destroyed planet, Rahab, which is thought to have been the home of an angelic civilization, perhaps Satan's home world. Rahab means boaster or pride. Beliefs are that it was the fifth planet out, where the asteroid belt is now located.

> *The pillars of heaven are stunned at His rebuke. He quiets The sea with his power, and by his understanding He shatters (maw-khats, dashes asunder),*
>
> *Rahab, by His spirit the heavens were beautiful; His hand forbids the fugitive snake. (Job 26:11-13 KJV).*

On Earth, the same judgments are taking place. God is destroying cities that were created prior to Adam's existence. Rahab means boaster or pride.

Psalm 89:10 says,

"You have broken Rahab in pieces, as one slain: you have scattered your enemies with your mighty arm."

To quote another author, David Flynn:

> The planet of the "Covering Cherub" is still evident within the debris, asteroids and comets, which are strewn throughout our solar system. Significantly, these chunks of the rebel angel's planet, cosmic stones, have been used to mete out God's judgment throughout history.

God's judgment on the rebels continued as the incomprehensibly violent and genetically unlikely dinosaurs, the very image of the dragon. "That old serpent" was destroyed with another chunk of the rebel cherub's planet.

Perhaps, the best time frame for when this happened would be during what we now call the Late Heavy Bombardment Period, which was approximately 4.1 to 3.8 billion years ago.

During this time, a large number of impact craters were formed on the Moon (also by inference), on Earth, Mercury, Venus, and Mars from the breakup of the planet within the asteroid belt, Rahab. Evidence for such an event comes from the dating of lunar samples that indicate most impact rocks formed in this narrow time interval. As seen in Genesis 1:2, the solar system was damaged beyond any self-repair. Earth alone received 22,000 impact craters, and several of them had diameters larger than 5,000 miles. What is now known as the Caribbean is in actuality a geologic structure from that era. The Earth became a formless void and the solar system was damaged by means of these great rocks from Rahab's judgment.

Astronomers agree that the Solar System has always had four giant planets; Jupiter, Saturn, Neptune and Uranus. Current claims are that it is much more likely to have been home to a fifth giant planet (no longer in the Solar System), of which remnants are now the asteroid belt.

Computer simulations by the Southwest Research Institute in San Antonio, Texas, show that it is statistically and extremely unlikely that the solar system began with four giants.

By their calculations, it only had a 2.5 per cent chance of reaching its current population and orbital layout with four giants. However, it was 10 times more probable to develop into its present state if there was a fifth monster body in the mix. In order to reach these conclusions, they ran 6,000 simulations of the Solar System's birth and early development.

Rahab was once a planet, like Earth but larger, that orbited the sun. The similarity was more along the lines of Saturn and Rahab's mass was large enough to hold ten Earths, plus it had a nearly circular orbit. Those remains are now the asteroid belt, as just discussed.

The asteroid belt is only a small remainder of the planet Rahab that once resided in the region between Mars and Jupiter. However, after Rahab met its destruction, gravitation and interactions with other worlds caused most of the mass to be lost in the rest of the Solar System and space. This also explains the moons within the Solar System. The moons, the rings of matter around the gas planets Jupiter, Uranus, Saturn and Neptune are leftovers of Rahab.

Due to their very strong gravitation, the planets Jupiter and Saturn attracted most of Rahab's non-gaseous matter.

Uranus and Neptune also magnetized debris and incorporated it into their planetary systems.

    Meteors and comets provide another argument in favor of a destroyed planet. Comets cannot date back to the beginning of the Solar System. This is because they consist of evolved matter such as water, which cannot form in the void of space. Water can only result on the surface of a planet with an atmosphere. In addition, comets often have rocks in their core. Meteors are debris from Rahab's crust that was blown away by the destruction, deeply into space, but the sun's gravity forced them to come back in an irregular orbit.

    With Lucifer's rebellion, death and corruption began to pervade the cosmos under his rule. Because he was the ruler of the whole creation under heaven, when he was cut down, all things were subjected to corruption and death. The ancient cosmos had the judgment of death upon it. Over the geologic ages, the universe and all things in it began to decay.

Many readers will question these statements, thinking that death first came into existence in the Garden of Eden with Adam's fall. Regardless, Satan's fall was before Adam because when Satan approached Adam and Eve, he was already a fallen angel and had to use the body of a snake to tempt Eve. Again, the only possible explanation is that Lucifer's fall was before the re-creation of the earth; otherwise, it would have been recorded as happening during Adam's time.

Romans 5:12 says,

"Wherefore, as by one man sin entered into the world, and death by sin; and so death passed upon all men, for that all have sinned."

This passage does not prove there was no death in the world before Adam sinned, neither does it rule out a Pre-Adamite world and its subsequent destruction. It merely means that Adam brought sin and death to himself as well as his offspring. However, nothing is said about any Pre-Adamite beings that may have preceded Adam.

The Greek word translated here as world is kosmos, meaning the earth and its inhabitants. In other words, kosmos is a "people" or "social system."

Adam caused sin and death in the world, or social system of humanity, but it is irrelevant in regards to another world or social system of Pre-Adamites.

Corinthian 15:21-22 says,

"For since by man came death, by man came also the resurrection of the dead. For as in Adam all die, even so in Christ shall all be made alive"

Again, this scriptural passage does not prohibit the creation and destruction of a Pre-Adamite world; it simply states that Adam brought sin and death to humanity. The reader should now be able to grasp why Elohim fashioned a Garden for Adam.

THE FIRMAMENT

"And Elohim said, Let there be **(hâyâh)** *light: and there was light." (Gen 1:3 OJB)*

Neither here nor in Genesis 1:14-18, is an original creative act implied. A different word is used. Light was the first thing made out of the dark chaos. In 2 Corinthians 4:4, the Apostle tells that out of darkness Light shall shine. The first order of business was to bring light into being as a means to remove one of the effects of judgment, *"darkness* **(chôshek)** *upon the face of the deep."* This was not the making of the sun, which is seen in a later verse, but the calling forth of light from the primordial darkness.

> *And Elohim said, Let there be a **raki'a (expanse, dome, firmament)** in the midst of the **mayim (waters)**, and let it divide the **mayim** from the **mayim**. And Elohim made the **raki'a**, and divided the waters under the **raki'a** from the waters which were above the **raki'a**; and it was so. And Elohim called the **raki'a Shomayim (Heaven)**. And the **erev** and the **boker** were **Yom Sheni (Day Two, the Second Day)**.* (Gen. 1:6-8 OJB)

The full meanings of these verses go well beyond any simplistic interpretation of the sky or outer space. A large part of the water was raised, leaving a space between it and the water which remained on Earth. Here, Elohim stretched out the heavens (râqîyaʽ - **spread out by beating, as gold leaf**). During the transition, some air was provided for the lower part of the heavens, yet on another day the starry bodies were created. They were in the firmament (Genesis 1:4) but the waters, which were raised, were above the firmament. Therefore, if this is taken as literal, the waters above the sphere are not water vapor, clouds, nor a canopy of water positioned above the surface. Instead, these waters exist at a great distance beyond the stars and not necessarily in a liquid form. Heaven was above the higher "Sea" and below the Throne of God.

Revelation says, *"And before the throne there was a **sea** of glass like unto crystal: and in the midst of the throne, and round about the throne, were four beasts full of eyes before and behind."* (Revelation 4:6)

Hence, this particular "Sea" above the firmament is higher than what is now known as the physical universe. Since the sun, moon and stars are in the firmament this "Sea" is above it. This interprettation of the sea being above the heavens is not rigidly offered, one only hopes that the reader will consider this explanation and give it some thought.

> *And Elohim said, Let there be lights in the raki'a of the heaven to divide the day from the night; and let them be for **otot** (**signs**), and for **mo'adim** (**seasons**), and for yamim (days), and shanim (years);* (Genesis 1:14 OJB)

In the writings of virtually all mythology a description exists of the major constellations, which are called the "Twelve Signs of the Zodiac." The story of redemption was told in the beginning of creation by the Zodiac and all ancient cultures, starting with the Sumerians, were aware of this astrological assemblage.

Within the book of Job, the oldest book of the Bible, God says,

Canst thou bind the sweet influences of Pleiades, or loose the bands of Orion? Canst thou bring forth Mazzaroth in his season? Or canst thou guide Arcturus with his sons? (Job 38:31-32 KJV).

Clearly, this references the constellations of Orion and Pleiades as well as the star Arcturus. Mazzaroth is the ancient Hebrew name for the Zodiac. In the beginning, there was a God-given Gospel in the stars but it is corrupted now.

The Zodiac was created to show the Gospel via the stars, along with "things to come." Josephus said that according to Jewish tradition, the Gospel in the stars was told by Adam, Seth, and Enoch. However, here is where the corruption in truth of the redemption story through the stars begins.

"Semjaza taught enchantments, and root-cuttings, Armaros the resolving of enchantments, Baraqijal (taught) astrology, Kokabel the constellations" (1Enoch 8:3)

The fallen angels, after the fall of man taught astrology and renamed the constellations and stars to pervert the truth told in the Mazzaroth.

The verse below tells us that the heavens still declare, "His eternal power and divine nature."

"For since the creation of the world his invisible attributes -- his eternal power and divine nature -- have been clearly seen, because they are understood through what has been made. So people are without excuse." (Romans 1:20 Net)

In the following verses, see that Elohim creates the seed bearing plants and animals, "after their kind" and says it is good.

And G-d said, Hinei, I have given you every herb bearing seed, which is upon the face of kol ha'aretz (all the earth), and every etz (tree), in the which is the fruit of a tree yielding seed; to you it shall be for food. And to every beast of the earth, and to every fowl of the air, and to every thing that creepeth upon the earth, wherein there is life, I have given every green herb for food; and it was so. And G-d saw every thing that He had made, and, behold, it was tov me'od (very good). And the erev and the boker were Yom Shishi (Day Six, the Sixth Day). (Gen 1:29-31 OJB)

During the Earth's earliest age, in pre-delugian times, a mist went up from the Earth and watered it (Genesis 2:5), which was before what is known as today's modern rain. The Earth did not receive rain until Noah's deluge when the great depths were opened up along with the giving of rain from the heavens. Confirmation of this exists in the Bible.

"But there went up a mist from the earth, and watered the whole face of the ground." (Gen 2:6)

MANKIND

I would like to quote the following passages from the Message Bible, and then look at the Hebrew and nuances of the passages. Genesis 1:26-27 declares:

> *God spoke: "Let us make human beings in our image, make them reflecting our nature So they can be responsible for the fish in the sea, the birds in the air, the cattle, And, yes, Earth itself, and every animal that moves on the face of Earth."*
>
> *God created human beings; he created them godlike, Reflecting God's nature. He created them male and female."*
> (Genesis 1:26-27 Message Bible)

Plainly stated, Elohim created man godlike, reflecting his nature. The question remains concerning what nature of Elohim man reflects.

> ***And God** ('ĕlôhîym) **said, Let us make** ('âśâh) **man** ('âdâm) **in our image** (tselem), **after our likeness** (dᵉmûth)..." **So God** ('ĕlôhîym) **created** (bârâ' - 'êth) **man** ('âdâm) **in his own image** (tselem), **in the image of God created** (bârâ') **he him; male** (zâkâr) **and female** (nᵉqêbâh) **created he them**.*" (Gen 1:27-27 Hebrew)

'âśâh – to make from pre-existing material (clay).

'âdâm – mankind in a general sense of humanity.

tselem – shade; a phantom, that is, (figuratively) illusion, resemblance. It is used of molten images; and of painted pictures of men. (Ezekiel 23:14)

dᵉmûth – resemblance, model, or shape.

bârâ' - 'êth – means to call forth out of nothingness. Ex nihilo the same "create" used in Gen. 1:1 meaning to create out of non-existent matter.

'êth - entity

zâkâr – remembered because all genealogy in the Bible traces from Adam, or the male of the family. This will be important to remember when we get in the third and fourth chapters.

    So what are we to take from this description of Elohim creating man in the first chapter of Genesis?

Notice from the description of Elohim creating man in the first chapter of Genesis that there was an inventive act by Elohim, which is not in question because the Hebrew word bârâ' was used.

In what why was man made in the likeness of Elohim? Man was made in the "image and likeness" of God, as seen in man's tri-unity and in his moral nature. Furthermore, it is evident in those things which are intrinsic to humans, such as laughter, because they are intrinsic to Elohim. Man is "spirit and soul" and body. Moreover, there seems to be a hint of man being made in a bodily resemblance of Elohim. Moreover, clues exist that humans were created with a bodily resemblance to Elohim.

In the opening words of the Gospel of John, that through Jesus, *"All things were made by him; and without him was not any thing made that was made."* (John 1:3 KJV) Thus, it is reasonable to assume that man was fashioned out of a resemblance to Jesus, and it is possible that he (Jesus) created man and walked in the garden as well.

> *And the LORD God (**Hashem Elohim**) formed (**yâtsar 'êth**) man (**'âdâm or ha adamah**) of the dust (**'âphâr**) of the ground (**'ădâmâh**),*

> *and breathed (**nâphach**) into his nostrils the breath of life (**nishmat chayyim**); and man (**adam**) became a living soul (**nefesh chayyah**). (Genesis 2:7 Hebrew)*

See here in the verse above the use of a dual name; "Hashem Elohim" or "Jehovah Elohim."

yâtsar 'eˆth - to mould into a form like a potter.

âdâm, ha adamah, - mankind as humanity.

ʿăphăr – clay, ruddy earth, the same root as Canaan.

'ădămăh – solid, redness.

nâphach – puff, inflate, blow.

nishmat chayyim - breath, divine, inspiration, intellect.

nefesh chayyah – alive, breathing creature.

By a creative act of Ex nihilo, man arose from the clay. The clay, by virtue of Divine omnipotence, shaped itself into Adam then he became a living soul. Man received his life through a distinct act of divine inbreathing of the Ruach Elohim, or Spirit of God.

Human form did not spring forth from the slime of primordial matter, but was created by Divine act. Man became a spirit having life. Although animals are said to have the breath of life, God did not breathe into their nostrils making them into living souls.

Man was, by his creation, in intimate fellowship with God, and developed out of the very substance and nature of Elohim. Due to this manner of design, all humans are God's children. Everyone pre-existed within Elohim's mind and immediately received life from him. Hence, man consists of a material substance and an immaterial substance, called spirit. Thus, Jehovah Elohim imparted some measure of his own spiritual nature to Adam.

Now, I understand that when you have one of the Godhead you have all three; however, we are going to talk about a theophany, or an appearance of Christ in a physical form before His birth. Jesus is described as the "*everlasting Father*" or, as it is better rendered, "*Father of eternity*". (Isaiah 9:6)

John 1:1-3 also states,

> *In the beginning was the Word, and the Word was with God, and the Word was*

God. The same was in the beginning with God. All things were made by him; and without him was not anything made that was made. (John 1:1-3 KJV)

EW Bullinger's translation of this verse is ideal.

"*In the beginning* [**of the ages**] *was* [**already pre-existent**] *the Word* [**Christ**], *and the Word was with God, and the Word was God*" (John 1:1EWB-CB).

Perhaps Jesus has always been the Elohim of the Old Testament, not that Elohim isn't three persons known as the Trinity (which is reveled in the NT), but that Jesus has always dealt with man. In addition, you might say if you have one, you have all three.

Jesus, in his pre-Incarnate form, breathed the Ruach Elohim into Adam. As a result, Adam became a "living soul." Imagine Christ reaching down and picking up a handful of clay (perhaps from the Temple Mount), and then breathing the "breath of life" into it.

Knowing that humankind would fall and He (Christ) would have to die for humanity would you have created a creature that you knew in your Divine knowledge would betray you? Moreover, knowing you would have to become the creature in order to save the creature, I dare say not! What a portrait of Divine love.

This is a true depiction of Divine love in action on the doorstep of humanity's creation. Some may never understand the incarnation, whereby God the Creator became man the creature! However, accept and believe that he did it. Suffice it to say, no one else would dare do what he did for his children!

The red dirt from which Adam was fashioned may signify the yod, which is the first letter of the name Jehovah. Furthermore, Canaan comes from the same root. According to E.W. Bullinger, Adam was created in Canaan and put in the Garden.

*"And the LORD God planted a garden in Eden [**delight**], eastward; and there **He put the man [Adam]** whom He had formed" (Genesis 2:8EWB-CB).*

Clearly, Adam was not created in the garden; he was put in the Garden. Lucifer had fallen prior to this event. He came into the garden and took over the serpent (according to most theologians). Therefore, it was necessary for Elohim to build a hedge-garden around his new creation. Garden in Hebrew means a protective hedge. I might add, if theologians are correct, then the hedge didn't work very well.

LIFE IN THE GARDEN

*"And the LORD God (**Jehovah Elohim**) planted a garden (**gan**) eastward in Eden; and there he put the man whom he had formed"* (Genesis 2:8 KJV).

Eden – Some versions translate it as Garden of Delight or Paradise of Pleasure. The whole earth was not Eden. Eden was a protected area. Most Bible scholars believe that the Garden of Eden was located somewhere within modern-day Iraq. However, the specific spot is not recorded. Because the existing Earth's surface was radically changed during Noah's Flood, none of today's maps can show Eden's original location.

The Lord created the Garden of Delight in the eastern part of the Earth towards the rising sun; it was a place beautifully planted with all manner of trees and filled with brilliant, dazzling scenery. In addition, the Lord made to spring up every tree, stunning to the gaze and superior for food. He placed there the tree of learning the knowledge of good and evil.

Genesis 2:15 tells that God commanded the man to "keep" the garden (gan). The Hebrew word shammar often translated as "keep," can also be interpreted as "guard" (keep safe). If man is to guard, there must be something to guard against.

The Garden of Delight was created to shield and protect Adam from the world around him because it had been subjected to sin and corruption by Lucifer's fall. The Hebrew word "gan" is translated as garden, but could be more accurately translated as a place protected by a fence. Although the world had been remade after its destruction, it was still subjected to Lucifer in some respects.

To the north of the garden, God created a river of water, clear and pure to the taste, unlike anything else. The water proceeded from the depths of the Earth and from the root of the Tree of Life; encircling the whole land of the Garden of Delight where there was gold, sapphire, and emerald. The water also divided itself into the rivers Geon, Tigris, and Euphrates.

Genesis 2:21-23:

> *And the LORD God caused a deep sleep to fall upon Adam, and he slept: and he took one of his ribs, and closed up the flesh instead thereof; And the rib, which*

> *the LORD God had taken from man, made he a woman, and brought her unto the man.*
> *And Adam said, This is now bone of my bones, and flesh of my flesh: she shall be called Woman, because she was taken out of Man.*

In the course of time, the Lord caused a deep slumber to fall upon Adam. Elohim then took one of Adam's ribs and created the woman (isha), that she might be a helpmeet for him. As such, one ponders if the serpent became jealous because he was not picked as Adam's helpmate. Perhaps the serpent had a particular hostility toward Eve, resulting in attacking her first.

After creating woman, the Lord awakened Adam out of his deep slumber. Upon Adams awaking, He brought the woman to him.

> *And God blessed them, and God said unto them, "Be fruitful, and multiply, and replenish **[refill, fill again]** the earth, and subdue it: and have dominion over the fish of the sea, and over the fowl of the air, and over every living thing that moveth upon the earth.* (Genesis 1:28 EW Bullinger Companion Bible)

Notice that this verse above seems a bit out of order, but for clarification, I put it in this order because it is more natural. More importantly, this scripture says that Adam and Eve should "replenish" the Earth. The word "replenish" literally means to "fill again" as it had once been filled; another proof of the Ruin-Reconstruction of the Earth.

*"And they were both naked (**'arum**), the man and his wife, and were not ashamed."* (Genesis 2:25 KJV)

Naked in Hebrew is 'arum, a homonym, which is the same word rendered as "subtil" in Genesis 3:1.

"Now the serpent was more subtil ('arum) than any beast of the field".

Now the question is what is Elohim trying to say? I suggest as some Extra-Biblical texts state that Adam and Eve were clothed in light, and perhaps the connection is that both Adam and the serpent were very beautiful.

The Hebrew word 'arum in Genesis 2:25 is best translated as "partially naked," meaning clothed in light. In contrast, Genesis 3:7 indicates a full nakedness is certainly meant, for *"their eyes are opened."*

They became fully observant that they were naked, whereas, they may not have known this earlier because of being clothed in light.

*"Now the Nachash was more arum (**cunning, crafty, wiley**) than any beast of the sadeh which Hashem Elohim had made. (Genesis 3:1 OJB)*

The story continues, after the conclusion of a very long period, maybe even a thousand years. No one knows how long Adam and Eve were in the Garden before the fall. Regardless, the serpent came and approached the woman then he said to her, "Hath not the Lord commanded you, saying, ye shall not eat of every tree of the garden?" Now can you see why Adam was told to guard the Garden?

Perhaps Satan spoke over the "hedge" to the serpent, or "possessed" the serpent as most theologians think. Could there be any other explanation? If the Garden was indeed designed to protect Adam, then it failed its mission.

The serpent was not a snake, as we know it today, although it was cursed to become one. The Scofield Bible says, "The serpent, in his Edenic form, is not to be thought of as a writhing reptile." That is the effect of the curse (Genesis 3:14).

According to the Hebrew Bible, the serpent was aw-room or subtle and beautiful, meaning he had intelligence with a cautious and clever character. In all of his cautiousness he was also the most beautiful of beasts. Moreover, he had intelligence with language.

We can assume that he often spoke with Adam and Eve. This familiarity would have created an environment where discretion was thrown to the wind. The Bible only recorded one of perhaps many conversations. Otherwise, common sense indicates that such a dialogue should have alerted Eve to something being extremely wrong.

> *But of the p'ri haEtz which is in the middle of the gan (garden), Elohim hath said, Ye shall not eat of it, neither shall ye touch it, lest ye die. And the* **Nachash** *said unto the isha, Ye shall not surely die (Genesis 3:3-4 OJB).*

Notice that the Nachash (Serpent) does not say, "Jehovah Elohim," implying a relationship to his creator, but just Elohim.

The Nachash was at the head of all inferior animals, and in a sort of intimacy with man as well as having had the gift of speech.

Oddly, most people are more willing to except that Satan engaged the Nachash (a lower creation), than consider that Adam (mankind) was duped by a lower creation. A point of debate certainly exists concerning how much lower. One no less than the great commentator, Adam Clark, stated that the Nachash walked erect and was in every respect formed like unto a man with the power of speech. This gives even more credence to my point that the Nachash wasn't a snake as we know them today, but cursed to become one, and my thoughts that the serpent may have been motivated by his jealousy of not being picked as Adams helpmeet.

"For God doth know that in the day ye eat thereof, then your eyes shall be opened, and ye shall be as gods, knowing good and evil" (Genesis 3:5 KJV).

It must be meant that Adam would then be like unto the "Elohim" or "gods" having a moral responsibility.

Sometimes Elohim is translated as the God, and sometimes as gods. This passage shows there had already been made a distinction between good and evil, although Adam and Eve were blind to it. It is knowledge that Adam and Eve desired, but it had been forbidden. Perhaps this was knowledge of morality.

This fruit of the tree of learning the knowledge of good and evil, though often portrayed as an apple was not an apple. The etymology of the words tree and fruit points to a sort of vine. Legend claims that the tree's fragrance extended to a considerable distance.

So what was the real temptation? What had Adam seen that he wanted? The temptation of the tree was to acquire a knowledge that Adam had seen with his eyes. What knowledge could have been seen or could have been displayed? Were there others in the Garden? Why was this knowledge forbidden to Adam? Adam and Eve sought to acquire a forbidden knowledge, something they saw displayed before them (Genesis 3:5). One wonders how knowledge can be displayed before a person as well as who were these "gods" that Adam & Eve could become like.

Perhaps angels (Watchers) were in the garden, along with Adam, and they had access to this tree. Maybe Eve was attracted to what she saw happen when they ate the fruit. The fruit of the forbidden tree could have been some sort of hallucinogen that caused the user to appear inebriated. Perhaps these Watchers also partook of this tree, yet Adam was prohibited to do so because of its effects and moral challenge.

Man's first temptation certainly was to partake of the tree; this displayed his ability to act in his own free will, outside that of Elohim. Knowing good and evil implied the right to exercise independent freedom in choosing between right and wrong. By partaking of the fruit, man set-up his moral order instead of the Lord's. Such action shows that God is not the author of sin. Man exercised free will and corrupted himself.

Sin is possible, even in pure beings, without the intervention of temptation. This is must be held as Scriptural doctrine. Hence man might have fallen, even had he not been tempted.

The "fall" is not so-named within the Bible. However, in Christian doctrine, it refers to the transition of the first humans from a state of innocence, to a state of guilt before God. Beliefs are that the fall corrupted the entire natural world, including humanity, resulting in people being born into a state of original sin. Such condition means that no one can attain eternal life except through the intervention of Jesus. His death served as a "ransom" by which humanity is offered freedom from the sin acquired at the fall.

Romans 5:12 speaks with the utmost clarity regarding the entrance of evil into this world.

It says, "*Therefore, just as through one man sin entered into the world, and death through sin, so death spread to all men, because all sinned*" (NSAB).

Now, you might have expected that the tempter would be introduced in quite a different way. It is evident that Lucifer has already fallen for the serpent seems to be the tool of Satan according to most theologians. Assume that sometime between Genesis 1:1 and Genesis 3:1, Lucifer fell.

As previously said, Ruin-Restoration Creationism provides the best evidence to this occurring between Genesis 1:1 and Genesis 1:2. The serpent has qualities that are superior to other animal life, such as, intellectual, communicative, and moral capacities. In addition, he is subordinate to Adam, a miniature monarch.

Note that the Pseudepigraphical Book of Jubilee gives all the animals the power of speech, but not moral capacities. Nevertheless, the Nachash had those characteristics; otherwise, Elohim would not have cursed the Nachash. Furthermore, the serpent is an animal and its descendants were included among the creatures that were allowed upon the Ark. However, it is the only animal ever mentioned which had moral capabilities.

Some of the Early Church Fathers follow the view that the Nachash had moral capabilities, such as Ephrem the Syrian. Many ponder why Elohim would have cursed the serpent other than that he had a moral responsibility. It is most evident in order to be cursed by Elohim, he must have exercised a free will of his own.

Evil was not invading on the back of a serpent who is one greater than humans. Rather, it was via a subordinate being from creation which chose evil in rebellion against Adam (his miniature sovereign).

Claiming that Satan is in the Genesis temptation is to assume something because the Biblical narrative does not state this to be the case. Due to the singular "thou" statements referring to the serpent, there is no allusion to another creature behind it. The following scripture says, "... *Because* ***thou*** *hast done this,* ***thou*** *art cursed ..."* *(Genesis 3:14 KJV)*

Let's continue by reading Genesis 3:6,

> *And when the* ***isha*** *saw that HaEtz was tov for food, and that it was pleasant to the eyes, and HaEtz to be desired to make one have seichel, she took of the p'ri thereof, and did eat, and gave also unto her ish with her; and he did eat' (Gen. 3:6 OJB).*

Notice that Adam's helpmeet was first called "**isha**." After the fall she was renamed Eve. Perhaps in view of the great redemptive promise, she is called the "the mother of all living."

Continuing on with the story:

> *And the eyes of them both were opened, and they knew that they were **eirummim (naked ones)**; and they sewed **aleh te'enah (fig leaves)** together, and made themselves **khagorot (loin covering girdles)**" (Gen 3:7 OJB).*

Khagorot – aprons.

Sin affected the way Adam and Eve perceived things. They lost their covering of light and literally realized that they were "eirum" (naked). Without their covering of light and purity of mind their first thoughts were that the Lord would see them naked.

Genesis 3:6 shows that Adam was with Eve when she partook of the fruit.

*"She took of the fruit thereof, and did eat, and gave also unto her **husband with her**; and he did eat."*

Therefore, Adam must have seen death overtake Eve, but chose to follow suit. Maybe this was because of his great love for her, or in defiance to the serpent.

A host of potential reasons exist as to why Eve's eyes may not have been opened until Adam ate. The obvious ones might be that they consumed the fruit so close to the same time that the difference was negligible, or possibly the effects were not immediate. Another explanation is that Adam was responsible for his wife, so that meant Adam would have had to fall in order for their eyes to be opened.

So what was it that they realized here? As discussed earlier, Adam and Eve lost their covering of light along with their innocence.

*"And they heard the **kol** of Hashem Elohim walking in the gan in the cool of the day; and HaAdam and his isha hid from the presence of Hashem Elohim amongst the etz hagan" (Genesis 3:8, OJB).*

Kol – voice.

Perhaps Hashem Elohim or Jehovah (Lord) God was in the habit of "walking" in the garden. This implies that Jehovah (instead of just Elohim, because of His connection with man) was bodily, like Adam, and had human appendages. Apparently, the Lord was accustomed to walking in the Garden. Theologians call this a theophany. I believe it to be a pre-incarnate appearance of Christ.

In the Hebrew one cannot tell, if this was Christ or all three. Conceivably, it was Christ alone. He is the one person of the Godhead who is most active in the redemption of mankind (remember the Trinity is shown in the New Testament to be three persons, Father, Son, Holy Spirit).

Note that nakedness was not a sin; however, their perception of it was associated with the act of disobedience. Even today, people all over the world wear clothes. In fact, individuals who do so are confirming the truth of God's word!

"And Hashem Elohim called unto HaAdam, and said unto him, Where art thou?" (Genesis 3:9, OJB).

HaAdam- Ha is always used to denote Adam as a person, not mankind in general. Surely, Elohim knew where Adam was located but called to him anyway for Adams sake. Maybe God asked, "Where are you?" in order for Adam to be aware of Elohim's presence. Incidentally, Adam replied,

*".... I heard Thy voice in the gan (**garden**), and I was afraid, because I was eirom (**naked**); and so I hid." (Genesis 3:10, OJB)*

In efforts to add a little bit of personal humor: A new pastor moved into town and went out evangelizing one day. All went well until he came to a certain house. He walked through the garden and knocked on the door. Obviously, someone was home because they moved a shade. Therefore, he knew, but no one came to the door even after he knocked several times. Finally, he took out his card and wrote Revelation 3:20 on the back of it:

"Behold I stand at the door and knock. If any man hears my voice, and opens the door, I will come in to him, and will dine with him, and he with me." He then stuck it in the door. The next day, as he was counting the offering after church, he found his card in the collection plate.

Below his message was the notation, Genesis 3:10 - "And he said, I heard thy voice in the garden, and I was afraid, because I was naked."

> *And He said, Who told thee that thou wast **eirom** (naked)? Hast thou eaten of **HaEtz**, which I commanded thee that thou not eat thereof? And HaAdam said, The isha whom Thou gavest to be with me, she gave me of HaEtz, and I did eat. And Hashem Elohim said unto the isha, What is this that thou hast done? And the isha said, The Nachash beguiled me, and I did eat (Genesis 3:11-13 OJB).*

Eirom- totally naked.

HaEtz- fruit of the Tree.

As seen earlier, HaAdam (Adam) was alongside the Isha (Woman) when she ate of the fruit and then gave to him. However, he was not beguiled or deceived by the serpent as the woman was so deceived.

> *And Hashem Elohim said unto the Nachash, Because thou hast done this, thou art arur (cursed) above kol habehemah, and above every beast of the*

> *sadeh; upon thy gakhon (belly) shalt thou go, and aphar shalt thou eat all the days of thy life; (Genesis 3:14 OJB)*

The Nachash (serpent) was cursed to go upon his belly. Perhaps, like the great commentator Adam Clark proposed, the Nachash originally walked upright as a human.

> *And I will put eivah **(enmity, personal hostility** [see Ezekiel 35:5]) between thee and HaIsha (see HaAlmah, Yeshayah 7:14), and between thy zera and her Zera; it shall crush thy rosh, and thou shalt strike his akev **(heel)**. Unto HaIsha He said (Genesis 3:15 OJB).*

God is speaking to the serpent who is perhaps a personification of Satan.

Elohim draws a distinction between "your seed" (Satan's seed) and "her Seed" (Jesus). "Her Seed" refers to the incarnation of Christ. Notice that this passage does not say that the "Seed" was of Adam; it is an inference to the virgin birth.

Thus, Genesis 3 is called the "Protoevangelium," which derives from Latin and means "first Gospel" coming from the word proto or protos. This interprets as first and evangelium referring to the Gospel.

This is the first prophecy of Christ's coming. Not only is this a prediction of his birth, but it is also a foretelling of his redemptive work. Elohim predicted the defeat of Lucifer by the cross of Christ.

Notably, Scripture speaks of placing one's foot over the enemy as a symbol of victory (Joshua 10:24–25; 2 Samuel 22:29; 1 Kings 5:3 and Psalms 18:38). Therefore, the reference need only imply a victory for the woman's seed at the cost of a serious wound from a defeated foe.

> *I will greatly multiply thy itzavon ([labor] pain) and thy childbearing; in pain thou shalt bring forth banim; and thy teshukah (longing, desire) shall be to thy husband, and he shall rule over thee. And unto Adam He said, Because thou paid heed unto the voice of thy isha, and hast eaten of HaEtz, of which I commanded thee, saying, Thou shalt not eat of it, arurah (cursed) is haadamah*

> *because of thee; in itzavon (pain, suffering) shalt thou eat of it all the days of thy life; Kotz also and dardar shall it bring forth to thee; and thou shalt eat the esev of the sadeh; In the sweat of thy brow shalt thou eat lechem, till thou return unto haadamah; for out of it wast thou taken; for aphar thou art, and unto aphar shalt thou return (Genesis 3:16-19 OJB).*

Adam and Eve are here along with the ground cursed. This is what some refer to as the original sin of eating the fruit being passed down from generation to generation, called the "sin nature." The ground it seems was cursed for Adam's best interest, although that might be hard to envision. Even the fact that man does not live forever is in the overall best interest of humanity because of man's rejection of God. Imagine 1,000 little Hitler's running around for an eternity; that would not be a good reality. Adam is told he was created from the dust and that to dust he would return.

*"And HaAdam called the shem of his isha Chavah (**Eve**); because she was the Em kol chai." (Genesis 3:20 OJB)*

Notice here Adam's helpmeet was first called "isha" then after the fall she was renamed Chavah (Eve). Perhaps because of the great redemptive promise she was to fulfill. Eve means, "The mother of all living."

"Unto Adam also and to his isha did Hashem Elohim make kesonos ohr, and clothed them." (Genesis 3:21 OJB)

Here is where the first blood sacrifice was performed by Elohim himself. Scripture later tells that without the shedding of blood there is no remission of sin. Therefore, at this point, Elohim's shedding of animal blood is in preparation for the coming of Christ as revealed by Genesis. This is certainly a look forward to Christ, typology or Protoevangelium in and of itself. Furthermore, it is a perfect description of God's redemptive work. He performs the sacrifice himself, provides it for man as an act of Grace, and clothes mankind with the skin of the sacrifice.

Let's continue our discussion:

> *And Hashem Elohim said, See, HaAdam is become like one of Us, knowing tov v'rah; and now, lest he put forth his yad, and take also of HaEtz HaChayyim, and eat, and chai l'olam **(live forever)**; Therefore Hashem Elohim sent him forth from the Gan Eden, to work haadamah from which place he was taken. So He drove out HaAdam; and He placed miKedem **(at the east)** of the Gan Eden HaKeruvim, and a flaming cherev which was ever-turning, to be shomer over the Derech Etz HaChayyim" (Genesis 3:22-24 OJB).*

In addition, the Targum says:

> And the Lord God said to the angels who minister before him, 'Behold, Adam was alone on the earth as I am alone in the heavens on high. From him there will arise those who will know how to distinguish between good and evil. If he had kept the commandments {which} I commanded him he would have lived and endured like the tree of life forever. But now, since he has not observed what I commanded him, let us decree against him, and let us banish him from the

Garden of Eden, before he puts forth his hand and takes {also} of the fruit of the tree of life. For behold, if he eats of it, he will live and endure forever (PS Jonathan).

Now lest at any time Adam stretches forth his hand and takes of the Tree of Life in order to eat and live forever, the Lord must send him out of the Garden of Delight. Therefore, Elohim forced Adam to leave the Garden of Delight and cultivate the ground out of which he was taken.

"On that day, the Lord closed the mouth of all beasts so that they could no longer speak, for they had all spoken one with another in the Hebrew tongue while in the Garden of Delight" (Book of Jubilees).

He sent out of the Garden of Delight all flesh that was in the Garden of Delight and scattered all flesh according to its kind unto the places that had been created for them.

Adam, passing out of the garden, must have passed by the tree of learning the knowledge of good and evil. Perhaps he saw the appearance of it. How perhaps it had changed, and how it had perhaps shriveled.

The Lord then barred Adam and Eve from the garden by an ever-turning, fiery, flaming, and sharp sword of the cherub lest they decide to return to the garden and eat of the Tree of Life. Upon being expelled from the garden, Adam looked back at the gate of the garden, and seeing the cherub with the sword of flashing fire in his hand, must have feared greatly.

CAIN AND ABLE

"And HaAdam knew Chavah (Eve) his isha; and she conceived, and bore Kayin (Cain), and said, Kaniti (I have acquired) ish with Hashem" (Genesis 4:1 OJB).

HaAdam "knew" Chavah means he recognized her nature and uses in a demonstrative sense, including sexually. The act mentioned here is recorded to indicate that paradise was not "without sex" (Jerome). This shows that while Adam was formed from the soil, and Eve from a rib taken out of his side, other members of the race were to be produced "from the union of a man and a woman" (Rungius).

In this statement much should be put to rest concerning Cain's birth. However, many argue that Eve conceived Cain from an affair with Lucifer. We didn't examine this in verse 3:15, because I wanted to examine it here where it is defeated clearly by the testimony of Elohim.

Unfortunately, many of today's Christian writers spread a false teaching that Cain was the son of the serpent.

This is called the Serpent Seed, dual seed or two-seed line doctrine, which is a controversial one. Contention exists because that dogma claims that the serpent in the Garden of Eden mated with Eve and Cain was the offspring of their union.

The "seed" of the serpent in verse 3:15 is not the seed or ancestry of Cain. This false belief is held by some adherents of churches with a radicalized theology (Christian Identity Movement) which promote a "Eurocentric" interpretation of Christianity. Advocates of this doctrine claim that the Jews, as descendants of Cain, are also descended from the serpent. Several supporters, such as William M. Branham (1909–1965) and Arnold Murray, teach serpent seed theology in a non-racial context. The best known are those teachers who are considered to be white supremacists.

In one variation of teaching, called British Israelism, allegations exist that many white Europeans are the literal descendants of the Israelites, through the ten tribes which were taken away into captivity by the armies of Assyria. Furthermore, it asserts that white European-Israelites are still God's chosen people and that modern Jews are neither Israelites nor Hebrews at all.

Moreover, it claims that they descended from people with Turco-Mongolian blood, or Khazars, or are descendants of the Biblical Esau-Edom who traded his birthright. Differences do exist between what groups believe, but the basic belief is that the original sin was an act of sexual intercourse between Adam and Eve.

Prior to that act, the serpent sexually seduced Eve; further, that Cain was conceived by that act. The doctrine that Eve mated with the serpent, or with Satan, to produce Cain was explicitly rejected as heresy by the early church father, Irenaeus, around 180 AD. A similar principle appeared in Jewish Midrashic texts during the 9th century and in the Targum of Pseudo Jonathan. Admittedly, this is considered a false doctrine by mainstream Protestant and Catholic theologians.

While on the subject of false teachings, one should also examine Lilith. In Jewish mythology, from the 8th–10th centuries onwards, there is mention of Lilith. She is said to be Adam's first wife and created at the same time as Adam from the dust of the Earth, in contrast to being created from his rib; this is only legend.

During the Middle Ages she became identified with succubae who would copulate with men in their sleep.

The only time the term Lilith was used in Scripture was in Isaiah 34:14, where it is a term used for demons of the night. Genesis of course mentions Adam and Eve, but -- please note -- doesn't mention Lilith.

> *And she again bare his brother Abel. And Abel was a keeper of sheep, but Cain was a tiller of the ground. And in process of time it came to pass, that Cain brought of the fruit of the ground an offering unto the LORD. And Abel, he also brought of the firstlings of his flock and of the fat thereof. And the LORD had respect unto Abel and to his offering: But unto Cain and to his offering he had not respect. And Cain was very wroth, and his countenance fell. And the LORD said unto Cain, Why art thou wroth? and why is thy countenance fallen? (Genesis 4:2-6, KJV)*

Eve gives birth to Abel. He became a shepherd (**hunter**) while Cain became a tiller of the ground (**farmer, gatherer**). Early mankind quickly divided into a social system of hunters and gatherers.

Perhaps *"And in process of time it came to pass"* meant at the end of the first year. Cain and Abel brought offerings to Hashem (Jehovah - Lord); Abel a sheep, and Cain the fruit of the ground. Hashem was displeased with Cain and his offering. However, *"Hashem had respect* (shâʻâh – **to gaze**) *unto Abel and to his offering"* probably means God consumed Abel's offering by fire from heaven.

Why would the Lord be displeased with Cain's offering? One possible explanation for why the Lord was displeased with Cain's offering is that it derived from cursed ground. Cain reasoned Hashem's displeasure with his offering and became angry. Hashem asked Cain why was he angry, not because the Lord did not know, but so that Cain might examine himself.

> *If thou doest well, shalt thou not be accepted? and if thou doest not well, a sin offering (***chaṭṭâʻâh chaṭṭâʻth***) lieth at the door. And unto thee is his desire, and thou shalt rule over him (Genesis 4:7 EWB-CB).*

This word "chaṭṭâʻâh chaṭṭâʻth" is often translated as sacrifice, hence it is translated here by E.W. Bullinger as a sin offering.

The Lord is in fact saying that forgiveness is available in the form of a sacrifice. Here is where both meanings are brought together. "*Sin lieth at the door,*" but also "*a sin-offering croucheth at the tent door.*" This confirms the correctness of Abel's offering, and God's way of escape from the sin crouching at the door.

Should Cain desire to avail himself of it, atonement awaits him, as God's forgiveness is for everyone. Cain just does not get it! In addition, as the firstborn, he could continue to have "preeminence" over his brother Abel, but only if he rid himself of sin by the sin offering. This is expressive of the condition that a slave has while under the bondage of a master.

We see here that God had established a system of sacrifice for sin. Even though this is not stated, it can be implied from the discussion in the verses above and E.W. Bullinger's translation of Genesis 4:16,

"And Cain went out from the Tabernacle placed by God for His worship."

Additional clarity to the story is as follows:

And Kayin talked with Hevel his brother; and it came to pass, when they were in the sadeh (field), that Kayin rose up against Hevel his brother, and killed him. And Hashem said unto Kayin, Where is Hevel thy brother? And he said, I know not; am I shomer achi (my brother's keeper)? And He said, What hast thou done? The voice of thy brother's dahm crieth unto Me from haadamah (Genesis 4:8-10 OJB).

The rabbinic sources teach that every person must recognize the inner conflicts that rage within one's soul; sinfulness becomes a personal reality whenever it is given into, and the feelings of guilt gradually become non-existent.

Although its negative influence is visible, giving in to sin produces a state of psychological and spiritual enslavement that is unseen to its victim. Thus, Cain rose up against his brother Abel and killed him; this is the first murder and explanation of it. Cain harbored pure jealously within his heart.

Notice that Satan is not mentioned anywhere in context of this act.

However, Jesus may have been referring to it in John 8:44 where it says, *"He was a murderer from the beginning"* (speaking of Satan).

> *And the Lord said unto him, Therefore whosoever slayeth Cain, vengeance shall be taken on him sevenfold. And the Lord set a mark (oth) upon Cain, lest any finding him should kill him* (Genesis 4:15 KJV).

Oth – mark or miraculous sign, or Elohim gave him a pledge.

A mark was put upon Cain to warn others that killing Cain would provoke the vengeance of God. Some interpretations view this as a physical mark, whereas other see the "mark" as a sign, and not a physical marking on Cain himself. That is, for Cain's protection. The Noahic Covenant (Gen. 9:6) was not yet enacted whereby God would require the death penalty for slaying another person.

The Targum of Jonathan says the sign was from the great and precious name, probably one of the letters of the word Yahweh.

The Talmud claims that it was the last Hebrew letter "taw" marked on his forehead, which signified his contrition. Rabbi Jose ben Hanan said that God made a horn grow out of Caine. He thought it was a horn that grew out from his forehead in order to warn people. This may have been where the "devil got his horns" in popular vernacular.

More modern interpretations allege that Cain's skin color changed or that the mark was actually a number (six hundred and sixty six); thus, foreshowing the Mark of the Beast in Revelation. The Bible does not clearly distinguish how to translate "oth" in this biblical context. However, most assuredly, the mark on Cain was not dark skin. The Hebrew Scriptures do not use "oth" anywhere as a reference to skin color. In addition, the curse was solely Cain's and not passed on to his descendants.

Cain left the land and became a vagabond.

> *And Cain knew his wife; and she conceived, and bare Enoch: and he builded a city, and called the name of the city, after the name of his son, Enoch* (Genesis 4:17, KJV).

Who did Cain marry and who was there to build a city? What should we say about Cain's wife's origins? Cain's wife and the inhabitants of his city must have come, prior to Adam, from pre-Adamite beings that lived in some vague era. Perhaps they even came from a competing creation of Lucifer. Some wonder if it is possible that Cain married a Neanderthal. Neanderthals were already here when God created Adam. They were not a part of God's creation!

No, God did not have to experiment! Evolution in the re-creation after Genesis 1:2 does not exist. However, it does exist in the first creation that was destroyed by God between Genesis 1:1 and 1:2; it appears this way in the geological strata. Jewish Talmudic and rabbinical tradition believes that before Adam was created, the world was more than once inhabited and more than once destroyed.

God's creation occurs in Genesis 2:7,

"And the Lord God formed man of the dust of the ground, and breathed into his nostrils the breath of life; and man became a living soul" (KJV).

Adam and his descendants were the only ones infused with the breath of God and a spiritual nature that corresponded to God himself. Noah's flood would have destroyed any remaining Neanderthal's, along with the line of Cain.

We now follow the descendants of Cain. It is common to interpret the descendants of Cain and Seth as representing the seed of the serpent and the seed of the woman; however that cannot be fully true. In the human drama "The Seed of Cain," there are parts of the human race which are opposed to God which are Cain's Seed and the Woman's Seed is Christ.

Cain named his first son Enoch, and the city he built after him. Unto Enoch was born Irad, who begat Mehujael. In addition, Mehujael begat Methusael. Furthermore, Methusael begat Lamech.

Lamech was the first polygamist; he had two wives. Although it is not condemned, polygamy is mentioned as an abnormality.

His speech (Genesis 4:23) was either bragging about a murder he had committed, or what he would do to anyone who crossed him. Maybe he was also trying to reassure his wives that they would not have to fear anything coming upon them by reason of what he had done or might do.

Enoch's offspring are those who are nomads, herders, musicians, and metal smiths. This chapter concludes with Eve bearing Seth and stating that, "God hath appointed me another seed instead of Abel," whom Cain slew.

GENERATIONS OF ADAM

At first I thought, this chapter was totally boring and superfluous, therefore, irrelevant. However, it provides a context that gives credibility to the Genesis narrative. This chapter is not an exhaustive revelation of persons born from Adam; it only includes those who descended from one another within Noah's direct line. Cain's offspring are not listed nor are Seth's collateral branches.

Adam lived 130 years prior to begetting Seth. He then lived another 800 years after Seth's birth, which means that Adam was 930 years old when he died (Genesis 5:3-5, KJV). Josephus says that Adam had 33 sons and 23 daughters. Regardless, this chapter does not discuss them all, only some.

Seth lived 807 years after he begat Enosh. He was 912 years old when he died. Thus, showing that Seth was 105 years old when Enosh was born (Genesis 5:6-8, KJV).

Enosh was 90 years old and begat Cainan. After Cainan's birth, Enosh lived 815 more years. His total lifespan equaled 905 years (Genesis 5:9-11, KJV).

Cainan was 70 years old when Mahalaleel was born. Furthermore, he lived 840 more years following Mahalaleel's birth; thus, confirming 910 as his age upon his death (Genesis 5:12-114, KJV).

Mahalaleel was 65 years old when he begat Jared. He lived 830 years after Jared was born. Clearly, Mahalaleel lived a total of 895 years (Genesis 5:15-17, KJV).

Jared is from the verb yaradh, meaning "shall come down." Suggestions are that this is an allusion to the "Sons of God" or Angels who "came down" to corrupt the daughters of men (in the next chapter). According to the pseudepigraphical Book of 1Enoch:

> *It came to pass when the children of men had multiplied that in those days were born unto them beautiful and comely daughters. And the angels, the children of the heaven, saw and lusted after them.... And they were in all two hundred; who descended in the **days of Jared** on the summit of Mount Hermon.*

The angels or "sons of god" descended in the days of Jared before the Flood upon Mt. Hermon.

Jared was 162 years old upon Enoch's birth. He then continued living 800 years longer. These numbers show that Jared was 962 years old when he died (Genesis 5:18-20, KJV).

At 65 years old, Enoch begat Methuselah. He then walked with God an additional 300 years after he had Methuselah. Enoch worshipped Elohim for 365 years and "he was not" for Elohim took him (Genesis 5:21-24, KJV). The New Testament says,

"By faith Enoch was translated that he should not see death; and was not found, because God had translated him: for before his translation he had this testimony, that he pleased God" (Hebrews 11:5, KJV).

Methuselah lived 187 years and begat Lamech. After having Lamech, Methuselah continued living 782 more years. He succumbed to death when he was 969 years old (Genesis 5:25-27, KJV).

Lamech thrived for 182 years before begetting Noah. All Lamech's days were equal to 777 years. This makes it evident that Lamech lived for 595 years after he begat Noah (Genesis 5:25-31, KJV).

Noah was 500 years old when he begat Shem, Ham, and Japheth (Genesis 5:32, KJV). Japheth was the eldest son. However, Shem was mentioned first because Elohim chose to use him in order to bring forth the Messiah.

SONS OF GOD

"And it came to pass, when HaAdam began to multiply on the face of ha'adamah, and banot were born unto them, That the bnei HaElohim saw the banot HaAdam that they were tovot; and they took them nashim of all which they chose." (Gen 6:1-2 OJB)

Have fallen angels in the ancient past mated with humankind? Mythology the world over would teach us that they have. This has been the kernel of truth behind the world's darkest myths. Furthermore, it has also been the basis behind mythological gods taking human women and creating demigods. In addition, it gives rise to a race of beings who built the Pyramids and Megaliths; the evidence of which is found in the tales, folklore, and traditions of many cultures around the world.

The Hebrew phrase translated as "sons of God" (בְּנֵי־הָאֱלֹהִים bene ha'Elohim) only occurs here in Genesis 6:2 and 6:4, plus Job 1:6, 2:1, and 38:7, where angels are clearly understood. In the Book of Job, the phrase clearly refers to angelic beings. Nowhere else is the phrase "sons of God" (בְּנֵי־הָאֱלֹהִים bene ha'Elohim) used.

A better understanding of the verse is, "the angels saw the daughters of." Literal translation of bene is "sons of." When used as bene ha'Elohim, it means members in the "category of Elohim" (gods). An example of such usage is found in the term "sons of the prophets" written as "bene ha'Elohim" (1 Kings 20:35, 2 Kings 2:3, 5, 7, and 15). On the other hand, Genesis indicates that the term (בְּנֵי־הָאֱלֹהִים bene ha'Elohim) is not referring to human beings. The contrast is drawn between bene ha'Elohim and benot ha'adam.

Some take "the daughters of man" to be the daughters of the Cainites only. However, it is sufficient to understand by this phrase, the daughters of man in general, without any distinction of a moral or spiritual kind, and therefore including both Cainite and Shethite females. "And they took them wives of all whom they chose. In the Hebrew this is written as, "the daughters of Adam" (aw-dawm') or benot ha adam. Now read the passage as, "The angels saw the daughters of Adam that they were fair," and "they took them nashim (wives) of all which they chose."

I like the way the Contemporary English Version translates these verses.

"The children of the supernatural beings who had married these women became famous heroes and warriors. They were called Nephilim and lived on the earth at that time and even later." Gen 6:4 (Contemporary English Version).

Three possible explanations exist for the usage of the term "sons of god" or "beney ha'Elohim" as found in the ancient Hebrew Scriptures. Nonetheless, only one interpretation fits the text of the Hebrew Bible.

The sons of God or (בְּנֵי־הָאֱלֹהִים bene ha'Elohim) are thought by some to be only the sons of Seth, and the daughters of men just the descendants of Cain. In this view, the crime was the marriage of the holy line of Seth to the unholy line of Cain.

The "son of Seth" interpretation appeared about 400 AD. This was the first dispute of the angel view, which a majority of Jews and Christians held prior to that time. Serious problems exist with this theory.

First, "the line of Seth" phrase is not defined anywhere in the Hebrew Bible as a holy line of people. Furthermore, the theory fails to take into account that history has not proven intermarriage among various cultures produce giants. Neither did the Lord destroy, nor threaten to annihilate, a race or culture due to interbreeding. In spite of modern day support of this concept, the argument is not convincing but purely a poor exegesis (analysis of text). Such interpretations are done incorrectly and only serve to prove one's own ideas.

All the early church fathers accepted the angel view. Those people included Justin Martyr, Irenaeus, Athenagoras, Tertullian, Lactantius, Eusebius, and Ambrose. They said, "The angels transgressed and were captivated by love of women and begat children who are called giants" (The Ante-Nicene Fathers, Volume 8, pages 85 and 273). Interpretations, other than angels, for the sons of God or beney ha'Elohim, only appeared after the fifth century.

The "sons of god" or beney ha'Elohim are thought by some to be mere rulers, and the "daughters of men" only the masses; the transgression in this view is polygamy.

Evidence for this theory is that rulers are often referred to as gods or the offspring of gods. Unfortunately, this is an even weaker interpretation. The problem with this theory is that royalty has never, including in the Hebrew Bible, been associated with deity.

The evidence for this view is that rulers are often referred to as gods or the offspring of gods. This is an even weaker interpretation. The problem with this theory is that royalty has not in any way now or in ancient times, or anywhere in the Hebrew Bible, been associated with deity.

Jude gives evidence in the New Testament for the angelic view. According to Jude, fallen angels, "*...in like manner [gave] themselves over to fornication, and [went] after strange flesh.*"

These other-worldly beings could take flesh upon themselves. Proof is in the fact that Abraham conversed with angels who appeared to him as humans while on their way to destroy Sodom. They even ate the food that he prepared for them. This is one of the most natural readings of the verse in light of the offspring being giants (Nephilim).

Additional proof of angels as the correct rendering of "sons of god" (בְנֵי־הָאֱלֹהִים bene ha'Elohim) in Genesis 6:2 simply shows that the Bible interprets the Bible.

If the phrase "sons of god" (בְנֵי־הָאֱלֹהִים bene ha'Elohim) is used elsewhere other than in Job 1:6, 2:1, and 38:7, it should be understood to keep the same meaning. Good Bible interpretation, or what is called exegesis, requires the same translation be given to the phrase when it is used in another place. Otherwise readers are not practicing sound Bible interpretation. They erroneously read something into the text that does not exist.

We also have the witness of the Septuagint where the "sons of god" are clearly defined as "Angels of God." "Sons of god" is clearly defined in the Septuagint Codex Alexandrinus. This is one of the earliest and most complete manuscripts of the Bible; it was written a little later than the Council of Nice (A.D. 325). The term "sons of god" is written in the Septuagint Codex Alexandrinus as, "hoi angeloi tou Theou" (the angels of God) and not as "hoi huioi tou Theou" (the sons of God).

And it came to pass, when men began to be numerous upon the earth, and daughters were born to them, that the angels of God (hoi huioi tou Theou) having seen the daughters of men that they were beautiful took to themselves wives of all whom they chose. (Septuagint Codex Alexandrinus)

It has been the opinion of Rabbinical Scholars, and the translators of the Septuagint that the "sons of God" or "bene ha'Elohim" were angels who cohabitated with Adam's daughters. The early church also agreed with this view. Justin Marty, Cyprian, Eusebius, and even Josephus (a historical writer) accepted this view. Justin Marty (earliest of the church fathers) accepted this view and championed it in his Second Apology.

This cohabitation with human females resulted in an offspring called "Nephilim." The King James Version says, "Giants." Those categories include the original Nephilim, Elouid, and Eloj. The original Nephilim begot the Elouid, to whom in turn, were born the Eloj (Book of Enoch, vii. 2).

This mingling was disastrous for humanity. The mingling of angel and human is a fact reported somewhat as a matter of fact in Genesis.

Angels can change into physical form even though by nature they are spirit beings. That these other worldly beings could take upon themselves flesh is clearly evidenced by Abraham's conversation with angels on their way to destroy Sodom who appeared as humans and even eat food. The Bible does not tell us how this happens, but it refers to angels *"...which kept not their first estate, but left their own habitation..."* (Jude 6-7 KJV). Jude gives us an understanding of fallen angels and their interactions with humanity and of those who resist such knowledge are called, "brute beasts" (Jude: 10 KJV).

Notably, the New Testament said that angels do not marry. This does not mean they are incapable of marriage or that they have never participated in it. Furthermore, the New Testament refers to the honorable angels, not wicked ones. The point here is that people will not marry in heaven. Jesus is not illuminating the sexual activities of angels and the institution of marriage is not necessary in heaven.

It surely appears bizarre to some people that the Bible contains a statement referring to fallen angels sexually interacting with human women and having children with them. However, the placement of these passages (before the Flood narrative) signifies that such behavior set the tone for, and contributed to, human immorality.

> *"And the LORD said, My spirit shall not always **strive** with man, for that he also is flesh: yet his days shall be an hundred and twenty years."* (Genesis 6:3)

The word **strive** is a verb form of the Hebrew word din, meaning "to judge," and is translated as "strive." However, in this case one expects the form to be "yadin". The Greek translation of the Old Testament has "remain with," a rendering which may find support to possibly understand ruakh as a reference to the divine life-giving spirit or breath, rather than the Lord's personal Spirit. Brenton's English Septuagint renders the verb as, "not remain among." Moreover, in this verse the word "men" is generic as it is in verse four when it is translated as "men of renown."

Admittedly, the Net translation most closely approximates the verse's true meaning. The Net reveals that the Lord said,

"My spirit will not remain in humankind indefinitely, since they are mortal. They will remain for 120 more years." (Genesis 6:3,Net)

Some have interpreted this to mean that the age expectancy of mankind from this point on would be 120 years. However, it is more likely that this refers to the time remaining between this announcement of judgment and the coming of the Noah's flood.

> *There were Nephilim in the earth in the days of Noah;* ***after their destruction by the Flood, as well as before it****, when the angels came in unto the daughters of men, and they bare children to them, the same became mighty men which were of old, men of renown. (Genesis 6:4EWB-CB)*

This cohabitation with human female's, mentioned in verses one and two, resulted in an offspring called in the Hebrew, "Nephilim." Giants in the Hebrew text are described as those "who ruined the world" (by their violence, (Enoch vii. 3, 4).

The text states that the Nephilim are the result of the intermarriage between the "sons of god" and the "daughters of man."

The Nephilim (giants/mighty men) are the product of this angelic/human cohabitation. What about the origin of the word Nephilim? When the ancient Greek version of the Septuagint was written, the word "Nephilim" was translated as gegenes (giant); thus implying "Earth born." This same terminology was used to describe the Greek "gods". Greek and Roman mythology have legends of "gods" coming down and intermarrying with humans having hybrids, half-human and half-god or animal. Unger's Bible dictionary explains that Nephilim are considered by many as demigods, the unnatural offspring of the daughters of men mortal women in cohabitation with "the sons of god" (angels). This utterly unnatural union, violating God's created order of being, was such a shocking abnormality as to necessitate the worldwide judgment of the flood" (page 788).

> And they [the women] bore to them [the Watchers] three races–first, the great giants. The giants brought forth the Naphelim, and the Naphelim brought forth the Elioud.

And they existed, increasing in power according to their greatness. (Book of Jubilees)

What most authors have not taken into account is that Nephilim and their children the Elouid, could reproduce. This explains some of the strangeness of ancient mythology. Nothing in the Bible or history indicates that Nephilim were sterile (unable to reproduce). Why would we think that they were sterile? They are referred to as "men," therefore, they were human enough to reproduce. Without an articulated exception, it must be assumed that all "men" are able to reproduce. The Bible calls Giants the "men of renown" in Genesis. Thus, as explained, if they were men then they could reproduce.

Note the words "and also after that." This probably tells of two "irruptions" by Satan's Fallen Angels. One was before Noah's Flood and another was after the flood when the Israelites came into Canaan land.

The Rabbis hold that these giants had seven names, which include Emim, because whoever saw one of them was seized with terror, "Rephaim," because their sight made people "soft" (fearful) like wax.

"Gibborim," because their brains alone measured 18 ells, " Zamzummim," because they inspired fear and were fierce warriors, " Anakim," because they wore huge necklaces in great numbers, " Avim," because they destroyed the world and were themselves destroyed, "Nefilim," because they caused the world to fall and fell themselves (Ber R xxvii). This is the kind of race, which makes plausible and understandable explanations of the many early megaliths, and structures, such as the ancient Egyptian Pyramids.

The Babylonians, Greeks, Romans, and all ancient cultures recorded a race of beings displaying great powers of intellect, huge size and great strength. These Nephilim were huge, and they not only had great strength, but since they contained genes that were a mix of fallen angels and humans, they had traits of fallen angels, such as strength, and angelic abilities which became in misuse occult powers.

> *And GOD saw that the wickedness of **man** was great in the earth, and that every imagination (purpose or work) of the thoughts of his heart was only evil continually.*

> *And it repented the LORD that he had made **man** on the earth, and it grieved him at his heart. And the LORD said, I will destroy **man** whom I have created from the face of the earth; both **man**, and beast, and the creeping thing, and the fowls of the air; for it repenteth me that I have made them (Genesis 6:5-7, KJV).*

The word "man" in this verse is generic as it is in verse four when it is translated as "men of renown" referring to the Nephilim. This verse is stating that both men and Nephilim would be destroyed by the Flood due to their evil. All life before the Lord in who was the "breath of life" would be destroyed. There are fairy-tail myths related to the hollow earth theory which presumes that some Nephilim were able to hide in the earth and thus avoid perishing. However, this is nothing but fanciful musings on the part of those who hold such views. The Bible nor the Book of Enoch teach any such preposterous stories. Here, it is important to understand that mankind, the Nephilim, and "all flesh" had corrupted its way upon the earth.

> *And God looked upon the earth, and, behold, it was corrupt; for all flesh had corrupted his way upon the earth.*

> *And God said unto Noah, The end of all flesh is come before me; for the earth is filled with violence through them; and, behold, I will destroy them with the earth* (Genesis 6:12-13 KJV).

As such, complete ruin overtook the creatures that were upon the Earth. This happened through the genetic interbreeding of the Nephilim (and perhaps according to the Book of Jasher even the mixing of genes) and the "sons of God" with all species upon the earth. Such is a glimpse of how horrid things became and the degree of violence that was perpetuated upon the Earth.

The very fact is we are told in the next verse that Noah's line is the only one that hasn't interbreed with a "son of God", a Nephilim, or one of their offspring. Understandably, this is shocking to most people. However, the text is clear and more of it will be examined in the next chapter.

NOAH

*"THESE are THE GENERATIONS OF NOAH: Noah was a just man and without blemish **(tamim)** as to breed and pedigree in his contemporaries, and Noah walked habitually with God."* (Genesis 6:9 EWB-CB)

Remember, we were talking about genetics, linage, pedigree, and the genealogy of Noah being uncorrupted, when all other lines of flesh had been corrupted. The Bible here uses the word "**tamim**" to describe Noah's pedigree. This is the same word used to describe the requirement of the sacrificial lamb to be "tamim" – without spot or blemish.

E.W. Bullinger's translation makes it very understandable as to what is being meant here when the word "tamim" is used. It is Noah's pedigree. This is important because all other lines had become corrupted with the interbreeding of angles and hybrids. Elohim was not going to destroy the world and then start over with a corrupted genome. Noah was righteous before Elohim and the sentence gives significant weight upon righteousness and pedigree as both were important.

It is important to understand what the world looked like prior to the Flood. The antediluvian (or pre-diluvian, pre-Flood) world is referred to in the Bible; this is a period between the Creation of the Earth and the Deluge (Flood) in the biblical cosmology. No one knows how many people were living at this time, but a guess might be made based upon Scripture.

According to calculations by Henry Morris, the total amount of inhabitants was approximately 10 billion people (The Biblical Basis for Modern Science, Baker Book House, 1984, p. 417). Admittedly, 10 billion is an astronomical number when compared to today's population, which is around 7 billion. Logistical problems arise in feeding and caring for a population over a billion. Therefore, maintaining such masses require a higher level of technology than what we currently give the pre-Flood world credit for having obtained. Should the population estimates be correct at nearly 10 billion, it would require similar technology as we have today including refrigerated shipping, reliable communications, and sophisticated farming methods.

The antediluvian world had a written language. We read of the "book" of the generations of Adam in Genesis 5. The antediluvian world also developed musical instruments, and metal-working tools. The antediluvian world was perhaps in the beginning a golden age. It also would have had a much larger land surface than today.

All of the continents of today were at one time a single supercontinent called "Pangaea" before later breaking up and drifting to their present locations. Evidence for Pangaea includes the presence of similar and identical fossil species on continents that are now great distances apart. It could have been in the days of Peleg (Gen.10:25) that this supercontinent Pangaea began to break up and drift apart, because the Bible says about these days of Peleg, *"For in his days was the earth divided."*

> *And Noah begat three sons, Shem, Ham, and Japheth. Ha'aretz also was corrupt before HaElohim, and ha'aretz was filled with* **chamas** *(violence). And Elohim looked upon ha'aretz, and, hinei, it was corrupt; for kol basar had corrupted his derech upon ha'aretz. And Elohim said unto Noach, The ketz (end) of kol basar is*

come before Me; for ha'aretz is filled with **chamas because of them; and, hineni**, *I will destroy them with ha'aretz (Gen 6:10-13OJB).*

Notice this Hebrew word **"chamas"** it stood out to me as being noteworthy. It is the Hebrew word we translate as "violence". But we might be missing something here. In pronunciation, it is very similar to the Greek word "chimaera." The close spelling of the Hebrew word for violence is obvious. Chimaeras in Greek mythology were monstrous hybrids. This gives even more credence and understanding to the fact that the world was filled with hybrids which corrupted mankind's morals and genetics; thus, leading Elohim to destroy the world.

The morphological image used of Elohim in relation to this universal corruption strikes every one as extraordinary. "*It repented the Lord that He had made man on the earth, and it grieved Him at His heart.*" This is what we call anthropomorphism, the attributing to God a personification of terms applicable only to man.

We are told that God is not a man, thus it is anthropomorphism when we say it "Grieved Him at His Heart." The Bible uses these anthropomorphisms that we might understand a non-understandable God.

The Latin's used the term "deus absconditus" to refer to a "hidden God", but God clearly reveals himself to us by the use of these human terms so that we can understand Elohim in our own terms. By "repent," we are to understand not that Elohim changed His mind, but changed His purpose only, with reference to mankind. Elohim decided that there was only one thing to do which was to wipe out the entire race of man (a generic term including Nephilim) and make a new beginning in Noah.

Many have argued the extent of the Great Flood. I believe it to have been worldwide. Why, because the world at this time was one supercontinent.

> *And, behold, I, even I, do bring a flood of waters upon the earth, to destroy all flesh [every kind of being], wherein is the breath [spirit] of life, from under heaven; and every thing that is in the earth shall expire* (Genesis 6:17 KJV).

If all flesh was to be destroyed (in whom was life), then the Flood would have had to cover all of the Earth. Otherwise Nephilim, people, hybrids, and animals would simply have migrated to dry land and avoided being destroyed.

Very simply put, he said what he meant, and he meant what he said. Therefore, as written,

"...the fountains of the "great deep" and the "windows of heaven were opened" (Genesis 7:11 KJV).

Thus, people can find sea shells and other marine fossils, including those of whales, in mountains all over the world. The Sierra, Alps, and Himalayas are some of the places where such things can be found. In fact, there are many references from ancient civilizations that speak of a worldwide flood. Hans Schindler Bellamy estimates that there are over 500 Flood legends in the world among ancient civilizations and tribes (Moons, Myths and Man, 1949).

Noah was the tenth of the pre-Flood Patriarchs. In his six-hundredth year, God sent the Flood. Noah died 350 years after the Flood, at the age of 950.

His descendants were Shem, Ham, and Japheth, from whom the nations branched out after the Flood. We see the maximum human lifespan, as depicted by the Bible, diminished rapidly thereafter.

THE FLOOD

*"Make thee an ark **(tebah)** [**a floating building**] of gopher wood; nests shalt thou make in the ark, and shalt coat it within and without with resin."* (Genesis 6:14 EWB-CB)

According to E.W. Bullinger, the Hebrew word "tebah" is best translated as a floating building. Moses, the author of Genesis, was raised in Egypt. Therefore he would have used the larger Egyptian cubit of about 20.5 inches. Some also speculate a cubit could be up to 25 inches.

God give Noah detailed instructions for building the ark. The requirements were that it had to have internal compartments (nests-rooms); plus, the total size had to be 300 cubits long, 50 wide, and 30 high. This put the ark at the size of a WW11 Heavy Cruiser! Some Heavy Cruisers had compliments of as many as 2,000 sailors. Realistically, the overall size of the Ark makes it the largest seagoing vessel known before the 20th century.

Gopher wood, from which the ark was built, is only used once in the Bible.

The word is of indeterminate origin, but some have noted similarity between the Hebrew letters g and k, suggesting that the word may actually be kopher, which is a Hebrew word meaning "pitch." Thus kopher wood would be pitched wood. Thou shalt "coat" or "pitch it" is the Hebrew word for "atonement" it is "kâphar." Hence, only an atonement kept back the waters of judgment

> *A window shalt thou make to the ark, and in a cubit shalt thou finish it above; and the **door of the ark** shalt thou set in the side thereof; with lower, second, and third stories shalt thou make it."*
> (Genesis 6:16)

Unfortunately, the Bible does not state the door's exact size. However, it is reasonably alleged to have been 10 cubits high, and eight broad. By some writers' views, that would be big enough for an elephant to enter through it. The door was so large that Noah, and those with him, could not shut it. This was done solely by the Lord Himself, thus, approving all those within the ark (Genesis 7:16, KJV).

> *But with thee will I establish My* **brit** *(covenant); and thou shalt come into the tevah (ark), thou, and thy banim, and thy isha, and the nashim of thy banim with thee"* (Gen 6:18, OJB).

Elohim tells Noah that he will create a "brit" or covenant with him. This covenant is explained in Genesis 9:11:

> *And I will establish my covenant (***brit***) with you; neither shall all flesh be cut off (*yikaret *-be cut off, violently killed) any more by the waters of a flood; neither shall there any more be a flood to destroy the earth.*

By this it is meant God will not destroy the earth again by a general deluge.

Traces of covenant-making are found worldwide and this custom originated with Elohim. The Hebrew word for covenant is "brit". The Vulgate translates "brit" as "testamentum", it means to cut or carve. Hence a covenant, from the custom of passing between the divided pieces of the victims slain on the occasion of making a solemn compact as seen in Genesis 15:19.

The first oath or covenant began with Elohim in the Garden of Eden. However, only the outlining of a covenant can be found. Nevertheless, there must have been the establishment of a covenant. Why a covenant because, neither Adam nor Eve seemed surprised that they were not to eat from the tree of the knowledge of good and evil. As in all covenants it was created by Elohim.

The second covenant was also created by Elohim and involved him killing an animal and shedding its blood to cover or atone for Adam and Eve's disobedience and resultant nakedness. Furthermore, the Noahic Covenant was created by Elohim, after God destroyed the earth with the Flood, and is instituted in Genesis 8 and 9. Among other things it established capital punishment, which happened after God destroyed the earth with the Flood. The sign of this covenant is the rainbow. God promises that he will never again destroy all life by a deluge, and creates the rainbow as a sign of His **"everlasting covenant"** for all ages to come.

> *And of every living thing of all flesh, two of every sort shalt thou bring into the ark, to keep them alive with thee; they shall be male and female. Of fowls after their kind, and of cattle after their kind, of every creeping thing of the earth after his kind, two of every sort shall come unto thee, to keep them alive. And take thou unto thee of all food that is eaten, and thou shalt gather it to thee; and it shall be for food for thee, and for them. Thus did Noah; according to all that God commanded him, so did he (Genesis 6:19-22 KJV).*

Clean animals, those acceptable for sacrifice, were brought into the Ark by sevens. Noah collected enough food for the animals for some period of time. Some commentators say Noah collected enough food for up to a year for all of the animals and his household.

"For yet seven days, and I will cause it to rain upon the earth forty days and forty nights; and every living substance that I have made will I destroy from off the face of the earth." (Genesis 7:4, KJV)

This was a literal forty days and forty nights, and as previously discussed, everything that had the "breath of life" died. A fanciful idea exists that some of the Nephilim avoided being destroyed by hiding in a hollow earth; however, that is only someone's overworked imagination.

*"And they that went in, went in male and female of all flesh, as God [**the Creator**] had commanded him: and the LORD [**Noah's Covenant-God**] shut him in."* (Genesis 7:16 EWB-CB)

Notice here that the, "**Lord shut him in**" *...with Shem, and Ham, and Japheth, the sons of Noah, and Noah's wife, and the three wives of his sons with them, into the ark*" (Genesis 7:13 KJV). By the fact that God shut the door, clearly he approved of Noah, Shem, Ham, Japheth, Noah's wife, and the three wives of his son's. There were no bad hybrid or Nephilim genes on the ark, period. When these Nephilim resurfaced at the time of the Israelite's entering into Canaan, it was from another incursion of fallen angels, not recessive genes on the ark. Anyone who knows anything about genetics knows that recessive genes become weaker over time in the general population, not stronger.

Therefore, Nephilim genes were not in the wives of Noah's sons and did not cause a recurrence of Nephilim on the earth; they came from another incursion (Numbers 13:33).

> *And the flood was forty days upon the earth; and the waters increased, and bare up the ark, and it was lift up above the earth. And the waters prevailed, and were increased greatly upon the earth; and the ark went upon the face of the waters. And the waters prevailed exceedingly upon the earth; and all the high hills, that were under the whole heaven, were covered. Fifteen cubits upward did the waters prevail; and the mountains were covered* (Genesis 7:17-20).

This was a worldwide flood which reached unto the tops of the mountains covering them with over 30 feet of water.

> *And all flesh ceased to breathe that moved upon the earth, both of fowl, and of cattle, and of beast, and of every creeping thing that creepeth upon the earth, and every man:*

> *All in whose nostrils was the breath of life, of all that was in the dry land, ceased to breathe. And every standing thing was wiped out which was upon the face of the ground, both man, and cattle, and the creeping things, and the fowl of the heaven; and they were wiped out from the earth: and Noah only remained alive, and they that were with him in the ark. And the waters prevailed upon the earth an hundred and fifty days* (Genesis 7:21-24).

All in whose nostrils was the breath of life, of all that was in the dry land, ceased to breathe. Every standing thing was wiped out which was upon the face of the ground, including any Nephilim and all humanity. No Nephilim hung onto the side of the ark, such as the far-fetched story of Org which is nothing but a myth.

> *And it came to pass in the six hundredth and first year [of Noah's life], in the first month, the first day of the month, the waters were dried up from off the earth: and Noah removed the covering of the ark, and looked, and, behold, the face of the ground was dry* (Genesis 8:13).

Noah first built an altar unto the LORD. He took of every clean beast as well as every clean fowl and offered burnt offerings on the altar. Elohim was well pleased with this sacrifice. The Bible states that, "the LORD smelled a sweet savour," indicating he was pleased. God blessed Noah and his sons and restated the Noahic Covenant.

And Noah was an husbandman [giving himself to tillage], and he planted a vineyard: And he drank of the wine, and was drunken; and he was uncovered within his tent. And Ham, the father of Canaan, saw the nakedness of his father, and told his two brethren without. And Shem and Japheth took a garment, and laid it upon both their shoulders, and went backward, and covered the nakedness of their father; and their faces were backward, and they saw not their father's nakedness. And Noah awoke [to wisdom] from his wine, and knew what his younger [than Japheth] son [Ham] had done unto him (Genesis 9:20-24 OJB)

What this terrible sin committed by Ham was we are not exactly told. It was one of either two things, it was homosexual in nature or Ham had relations with his mother (Leviticus 18:18).

Commentators are divided upon what Ham's sin was. Either way, it was demonically inspired. Many individuals, including myself, believe it was homosexual in nature. With the Flood as well as the destruction of the Nephilim and all manner of hybrids, these creatures became disembodied spirits that neither heaven nor hell was made to contain. Therefore, they continue walking on Earth and undoubtedly influenced Ham.

The Book of Enoch provides extra-biblical details and an expository retelling of the etiology for evil spirits. A case can be made for Enoch's advanced demonology whether one attributes its contents to a divine origin or a historical book written by men.

> *And now the giants, who have been begotten from body and flesh, will be called evil spirits on earth, and their dwelling-places will be upon the earth. Evil spirits proceed from their bodies; because they are created from above, their beginning and first basis being from the holy watchers, they will be evil spirits upon the earth, and will be called evil spirits. But the spirits of heaven have their dwelling-places in heaven, and the*

> *spirits of the earth, who were born on the earth, have their dwelling-places on earth. And the spirits of the giants, who cast themselves upon the clouds, will be destroyed and fall, and will battle and cause destruction on the earth, and do evil; they will take no kind of food, nor will they become thirsty, and they will be invisible."* (1Enoch 15: 8-11)

The Book of Enoch and the Bible tell us what became of these departed spirits of the Nephilim. The Nephilim became what we now know as "demons." This is seen in Lev. 17:7; Deut. 32:17; II Chron. 11:15; Psa. 106:37 and Job 26. Noah's flood destroyed the Nephilim bodies, but that left them as disembodied spirits looking for a body through which they might once again affect their evil ways. In the New Testament, they are called "demons," "unclean spirits," and "evil spirits". Undoubtedly, from the evilness of Ham's sin, he must have been influenced by them, the same as many are today.

"And he said, "Cursed be Canaan; a servant of servants shall he be unto his brethren." And he said, "Blessed be the LORD God of Shem; and Canaan shall be his servant." (Genesis 9:25-26 KJV)

Again, why Noah cursed Canaan instead of Ham we are not told. However, Canaan's curse was not to become black. I do not think the races came into being until the tower of Babel when God dispersed the nations. However, Canaan's curse was to become a slave and which slavery may have continued through his seed after the tower of Babel into the black nations that formed after the Tower of Babel.

*And Cush fathered Nimrod; he began to be a gibbor in ha'aretz. He was a gibbor, a hunter before Hashem; therefore it is said, like **Nimrod** the gibbor, the hunter before Hashem.* (Genesis 10:8-9, OJB)

There has been much written about Nimrod, and he was certainly an earlier forerunner of the Anti-Christ. I do not think he became a Nephilim in the since of a hybrid, but a "gibbor" in the sense of a mighty man of renown.

Furthermore, Nimrod was the great-grandson of Noah, the son of Cush, grandson of Ham and nephew of Canaan. He was the very first world ruler. It is believed that the anti-Christ will be just like him. In addition, some say Nimrod is the ancestor of the future anti-Christ, or that he will be raised from the dead; that is pure fiction because his bones long ago turned to dust.

The name Nimrod means "The Rebel" or "to rebel" and certainly suits him. He was a rebel. He was a tyrant, bully, treacherous and a dangerous individual who thought nothing of his cruel deeds. It is thought that he was the first to hunt men and perhaps the first to introduce slavery to humanity. However, he did establish great cities, including Babylon from which he ruled. In some extra-biblical traditions it is also said that he built the Tower of Babel. Nimrod is traditionally credited with building it in the land of Shinar, although the Bible never states this fact. Josephus wrote, "Now it was Nimrod who excited them to such an affront and contempt of God. He was the grandson of Ham, the son of Noah, a bold man, and of great strength of hand."

Nimrod persuaded people not to ascribe it to God as if it was through his means that they were happy, but to believe it was their own courage that procured happiness. Moreover, he gradually changed the government into tyranny, seeing no other way of turning men from the fear of God, but to bring them into a constant dependence on his own power. He also said that should God have a mind to drown the world again, then he would get revenge on him by building a tower that was too high for the waters to reach. Nimrod vowed to avenge himself on God for destroying their forefathers as well.

Now a multitude was very ready to follow Nimrod's determination, including esteeming it as cowardice to submit to God. They built a tower, neither sparing any pains nor being in any degree negligent about the work. By reason of the multitude of hands employed in it, the tower grew very high, sooner than anyone expected. Realistically, it was very thick and so strongly built that upon view its great height seemed to be less than the actual size. This structure consisted of burnt brick, cemented together with mortar and made of bitumen in order for it to resist water.

When God saw that they acted so madly, he did not resolve to destroy them utterly, since they were not grown wiser by the destruction of the former sinners. Instead, he created a tumult by putting diverse languages into them. Due to the variety of those languages, they could no longer understand one another like they had easily done in the past. Incidentally, the place where they built the tower is now called Babylon. This is because of the confusion that resulted from the language changes; in Hebrew, Babel means "confusion."

Nimrod also figures into some very early versions of the history of Freemasonry. He was said to have been one of the founders of Freemasonry.

TOWER OF BABEL

"And the whole earth was of one language, and of one speech. And it came to pass, as they journeyed from the east, that they found a plain in the land of Shinar; and they dwelt there. And they said one to another, Go to, let us make brick, and burn them throughly. And they had brick for stone, and slime had they for morter. And they said, Go to, let us build us a city and a tower, whose top may reach unto heaven; and let us make us a name, lest we be scattered abroad upon the face of the whole earth. And the LORD came down to see the city and the tower, which the children of men builded. And the LORD said, Behold, the people is one, and they have all one language; and this they begin to do: and now nothing will be restrained from them, which they have imagined to do. Go to, let us go down, and there confound their language, that they may not understand one another's speech. So the LORD scattered them abroad from thence upon the face of all the earth: and they left off to build the city.

Therefore is the name of it called Babel; because the LORD did there confound the language of all the earth: and from thence did the LORD scatter them abroad upon the face of all the earth."
(Genesis 11:1-9, KJV)

The account of the building of the Tower of Babel begins by saying that the world had one common language. This language was according to ancient texts Hebrew. The tower that figures predominantly in the narrative is to be identified as a ziggurat (stepped pyramid). Nearly thirty ziggurats in the area of Mesopotamia have been discovered by archaeologists.

Cleary, the Tower was somehow a threat and God put a stop to it. Scholars who study this subject now believe that the tower was more than just an extremely tall building; it was to be a portal, a doorway between other dimensions. Nimrod and Babylon's inhabitants were going to use it to access the spiritual realms. Commentators Schott and Vincent proposed the idea that the tower was the entrance door through which a god passed to the lower temple. This is clearly seen as a common theme in the names given to most of the ziggurats in southern Mesopotamia.

They were right; the tower may have been built to open a portal for fallen angels. If it were just a tall building Elohim would not have destroyed it and changed everyone's language. God was not going to allow them access to the spiritual realms. God simply put a stop to construction and confused their languages, causing them to leave and team up with others of their language and go and settle throughout the earth. They left speaking of what had just happened and about Nimrod. These stories were passed down from one generation to the next, each in their own language.

One point that has always stood out to me was the statement, "*...and now nothing will be restrained from them, which they have imagined to do.*" Did this include space travel, could man have gone to space thousands of years earlier? It seems here that Elohim has purposely held back man's ability to create technology. It may be that fallen angels are involved in some of mankind's darker technologies. It seems ancient man knew that there was some kind of limitation to accessing the spiritual realms. In building the Tower of Babel people might have been looking for a way to circumvent it.

Portals and the attempt to create them is nothing new; humanity has been about trying to create them since the Tower of Babel. However, legitimizing the search of such for them is entirely new. Emerging figures in Christendom are now seeking to create openings. There seems to be a rush to see who can outdo whom. What once was understood to be forbidden is now fast becoming legitimized by left-wing Christians. What they expect to step out of these event horizons is an interesting question. Some parts of the country even have modern-day groups that seek to open portals, thinking only good beings can come through the opening! They might be surprised!

Allegedly, the Greek historian Herodotus visited the tower in 460 BC, after the tower had been crumbling for many years. He wrote:

> It has a solid central tower, one furlong square, with a second erected on top of it and then a third, and so on up to eight. All eight towers can be climbed by a spiral way running around the outside, and about halfway up there are seats for those who make the journey to rest on. On the summit of the topmost tower stands a great temple with a fine large

couch in it, richly covered, and a golden table beside it. The shrine contains no image, and no one spends the night there except (if we may believe that Chaldaeans who are the priests of Bêl) one Babylonian woman, all alone, whoever it may be that the god has chosen. The Chaldaeans also say -though I do not believe them- that the god enters the temple in person and takes his rest upon the bed." [Herodotus, Histories 1.181-2]

No one knows for sure if this account is accurate. However, Herodotus is accurate in a lot of his writings.

Does this sound like what we talked about in Genesis the fourth chapter? Could the Tower of Babel have been built to accommodate unholy mating of fallen angles and humans?

AUTHORS BIOGRAPHY

I was born in a small, insignificant town in the southern part of the USA; so far south that they had to pipe in the sunshine! I was born in the month of April into a family of twelve in South Georgia on an island called Cumberland. April in the south warms as it recovers from mild winters and takes on a new life as azaleas bloom, porpoises frolic, and wild horses give birth to new colts. Cumberland is a wonderful place with its tidal pools, abundant wildlife, untouched sand dunes, deep forests, and history. Heck, around the turn of the century, we even had a bear! Ill not mention the alligators other than to say we had our share of them. But they're about as worthless as the sharks, of which Christmas Creek has an ample supply. My siblings and I explored the beaches and the forests on a daily basis.

Each of us learned to swim at the ripe young age of five by being thrown off the dock with a rope tied around the waist. Our father thought it was of the utmost importance that we learn to swim. I guess he was right, seeing that we lived on an island!

Perhaps the training method was a little harsh (I would not recommend it), but it was effective.

Somewhere around the time I had reached eight or so years of age, I experienced my first vision. One evening as I returned to my bedroom, a wall disappeared. Where the wall had been was a man sitting upon a stage. He sat in a chair at the edge of the stage, putting his hands upon the heads of those passing by beneath him. As I watched these people walk beneath him, he laid his hands upon them. I realized that the man was me, just older! It was obvious that I was in some kind of ministry. I thought all of this very unusual, because I had never seen anything like this. All I knew about ministry at this time was what I learned in the Methodist Church. You can rest assured nothing like this was going on in the Methodist Church in the 1960s.

I was by definition a tenacious child, but about what I did not know. In the early 1970s upon turning twelve, I took my first steps into business ownership; I built a shop in my parent's backyard and began repairing lawnmowers. It was a great income for a teenager, perhaps too good.

As with most coming-of-age young people, sin lurked at my doorstep and by 1977, I was an aspiring teenage alcoholic, complete with blackouts. Even at this tender age, the world had shown its web of deceit, lies, and drama.

I will always be indebted to a caring science teacher, whose name has been lost to time, for his introducing me to the living Christ. As most of us have heard of Christ, I had heard, having grown up, as I mentioned, in church. However, this humble man was the first person I had met who really seemed to have a relationship with this Jesus the God Man. I am sure there must have been other people like him with whom I had contact, but none that I knew seemed to have the kind of feelings exemplifying a real relationship with Jesus. I began to talk with him between classes. On one particular day, I meditated on a text of scripture in Ecclesiastes.

"Vanity of vanity, saith the Preacher, vanity of vanities, all is vanity" (Ecclesiastes 1:2).

I was moved by a war of sorts that seemed to be going on within me; it was as if evil was determined to drag my soul along with it. It literally was evil vying within me for my soul. It had the opposite effect.

You could say that it scared the hell out of me. I returned the next day to talk again with my teacher. I eagerly waited for the class to end, knowing I then would have time to speak about the struggle I had felt the night before in my soul. When the moment arrived, I dashed from my desk to where he stood.

I began to relate the struggle I had felt, and he asked me if I would pray and receive Christ. I wanted to but could not speak. I had become dumb; I was not able to open my mouth to speak in any manner! Seeming to understand this strange occurrence, he pointed directly at me and spoke commandingly to a devil, one that I could not see. He told the devil to go in the name of Jesus! Immediately I cried at the top of my voice, Jesus!

I knew not what to say, only crying out to Jesus, the one I knew who alone could rescue me from the war that had only moments ago rendered me unable to speak. As I heard myself cry out, I became aware of the darkness within my soul. It was as if I was looking inside of myself as some kind of spectator.

As I surveyed the vastness of this darkness, I became cognizant of the fact that in the middle of this vast darkness, there was a pinpoint of light beginning to expand at an ever-increasing velocity until it appeared as a supernova and burst forth out of every part of my being, leaving my extremities at what seemed to me to be the speed of light. I staggered a few feet and recovered my composure. I was stunned.

    I certainly had no point of reference for what I had just experienced. The years to come would, of course, show the vast changes that had occurred. I no longer was an alcoholic or an addict of any kind from that moment forward. I later learned that the old man had died and the new man had been born. I had been born again and would never be the same. Now, nearly four decades later, I can say it was the defining moment of my life.

If you have enjoyed this book, or it has had an impact on your life, we would like to hear from you.

****

CK Quarterman is available to speak at your function, church group, or meeting on any Bible subject.

If you would like CK Quarterman to join your discussion by phone, please include that in your request. He would be more than happy to join you for an hour by conference line.

Appointments are set on a first-come basis, and depend on availability.

For more information about

CK Quarterman

&

Genesis Secrets Revealed

Primeval

Please visit:

www.genesissecretsrevealed.com

ckquarterman@gmail.com

http://www.facebook.com/ckquarter

For more information about our book, *Fallen Angels: Giants, UFO Encounters, and the New World Order* please visit our website:
http://www.fallenangelstoday.com/

Made in the USA
Charleston, SC
29 November 2012